Dolley Madison

Books by Elswyth Thane

FICTION
Riders of the Wind
Echo Answers
Cloth of Gold
His Elizabeth
Bound to Happen
Queen's Folly
Tryst
Remember Today
From This Day Forward
Melody
Letter to a Stranger

THE WILLIAMSBURG NOVELS
Dawn's Early Light
Yankee Stranger
Ever After
The Light Heart
Kissing Kin
This Was Tomorrow
Homing

NONFICTION
The Tudor Wench
Young Mr. Disraeli
England Was an Island Once
The Bird Who Made Good
Reluctant Farmer
The Family Quarrel
Washington's Lady
Potomac Squire
Mount Vernon Is Ours
Mount Vernon: The Legacy
Mount Vernon Family
The Virginia Colony
Dolley Madison

PLAYS
The Tudor Wench
Young Mr. Disraeli

Elswyth Thane

Dolley
Madison

HER LIFE AND TIMES

CROWELL-COLLIER PRESS

Library of Congress Catalog Card Number: 77–108148

The Macmillan Company
866 Third Avenue
New York, New York 10022

Collier-Macmillan Canada Ltd., Toronto, Ontario

Printed in the United States of America

FIRST PRINTING

To
Elmer LaFlamme

Contents

Dolley Madison

1

A Quaker Girl

Dolley Payne came to Philadelphia with her family in the summer of 1783. She was just fourteen, and had spent most of her childhood on a plantation in Virginia called Scotchtown. This was a rambling, roomy house large enough for eight children and their parents. Dolley was the third child and the first daughter. Three sisters had followed her, and then two more brothers. She spelled her name with an *e* because that was the way it was written by the clerk in the register of the country parish in North Carolina where she was born while her parents were there on a visit. Not Dorothea, as was later supposed; Dolley, perhaps by her mother's wish, from her birth. Because she was required to be responsible for the younger ones as time went on, she was always a capable, good-natured girl, showing her Irish ancestry in her dark curls and blue eyes.

It was a Quaker family, arriving in the foremost Quaker city in America on the heels of a great war. Her parents had adopted the "plain" faith of the Society of Friends soon after their marriage, and like many converts her father was zealous in his observance of its many rules and regulations. In a day when men wore silver buckles on their shoes and knee-breeches, and a froth of lace at their throats and cuffs, there were none of these on John Payne's dark clothes. His hat was a flat, broad-brimmed beaver instead of the fashionable three-cornered tricorne edged with gilt lace. Quaker womenfolk wore drab, full-skirted dresses of gray, brown, or black stuff, with broad white collars at the high necks. In the street and at Meeting their faces were eclipsed by stiff black coal-scuttle bonnets which prevented them from seeing either to the right or left, like horses' blinders. Colored ribbons and jewelry were forbidden, and Dolley's first childish sorrow was said to be the accidental loss of some trinket such as a brooch or locket which had been smuggled into her possession by a frivolous non-Quaker grandmother, and which Dolley had worn secretly in a little cotton bag underneath her dress.

There was no music, either in church or in the Quaker homes, no card-games, no dancing-school for the children—no "vanities" or worldly diversions, to take the mind off the rule of the Spirit. In spite of which, even as a child Dolley wore every day a white linen mask made by her mother and fastened to the front of her bonnet to protect her delicate skin from the weather, and gloves to keep her hands smooth and white—small vanities which were doubtless maintained at the expense of her father's disapproval.

The luxury of good food was permitted, and the Paynes' table was always set as lavishly as their means could provide, although on the plainest of china and utensils. In conversation with each other and with strangers alike, they used the Quaker "thee" and "thou," a custom which arose from their conviction of human equality and which rejected the old language where "you" was a formality reserved for one's betters or a stranger who might be "quality." In some modern languages this distinction still exists, such as the French *"tu-toi"* between lovers and family, and *"vous"* for everyone else.

At the end of the Revolutionary War, in common with others of the Quaker faith, John Payne had developed "a concern" about slavery, and he joined with other Quakers at that time in a determination to free all his Negroes and henceforth run his household and earn his income by the sole efforts of himself and his numerous family. This decision caused some dismay, both among his womenfolk and his devoted servants. His wife and daughters were of course competent to cook and sew and clean the house, or could soon learn to be. But the question at once arose as to what was to become of the colored people who were accustomed to do all these chores for the family and who depended on him for support and occupation.

What arrangements Quaker John Payne was able to make for his Negro dependents, or how many of these there were at Scotchtown we do not know, except that his only capital was the few hundred dollars he had received for the sale of Scotchtown without its slaves. This he carried with him when he and his family left the comparative ease and comfort of plantation life for the more austere existence in the city of Philadelphia which his conscience dictated.

One member of the Scotchtown household refused to be left behind for any newfangled notion of the master's. The children's colored mammy, Amy, insisted on accompanying her darlings wherever they might be going, so that Payne gave in to her entreaties and the children's tears and included her in the move—with the understanding that thereafter she would receive monthly wages in return for the loving care she had always bestowed. Wages meant nothing to Amy. She was fed and housed and living with her people, which was all she wanted. When she died as an old woman in Philadelphia some years later, she left a little hoard to her mistress: all her wages, tucked away unspent—a very welcome legacy then to John Payne's much tried wife and daughters.

The Paynes were warmly welcomed to Philadelphia in 1783 by their friends the Drinkers, an established and prosperous Quaker family. Eliza Drinker's father and Mary Payne's were old acquaintances, and their children were soon close companions. After the twenty rooms at Scotchtown, there must have been some very inconvenient doubling up in the little two-story house with an attic on 3rd Street a few doors from the Drinkers in a row of identical brick houses, with graceful doorways and white marble doorsteps which were kept snowy clean by daily scrubbing.

John Payne in his first business venture invested unwisely in buying a starch business from its former owner who was retiring. It should have been a profitable enterprise, as starch was then in much demand and was used to size yarn, dress cloth, and thicken the colors in calico dyeing, as well as for laundering the gentlemen's shirts and ruffles and the ladies' petticoats. But somehow John Payne failed to prosper as a merchant, though he was more successful in Meeting, where he soon became an elder and a highly respected man. His eldest son Walter went to England to make his fortune, and never repaid the passage money to his father—never returned to America, it proved.

In 1783, when the Paynes arrived in Philadelphia, the war with England had ended at Yorktown in Virginia two years before—though the British army still occupied New York City, and the delegates at Paris were still wrangling out the terms of the peace treaty. Washington was at his camp on the Hudson with the remains of an army which was diminishing daily by desertion and was near to mutiny for lack of pay. A delegation of unruly soldiers demanding to be paid and allowed to go home had appeared in front of the Philadelphia State House in

June, before the Paynes left Virginia. The disorderly conduct of the soldiers so alarmed the Congress then sitting in the building that it had removed itself in a body to Princeton, New Jersey, where it was still camping out in some discomfort, but with a good deal of gaiety. Its absence was felt in Philadelphia trade and society, and added to the inevitable post-war depression.

But to country-bred Dolley the city was a fascinating show, with its carriage and stagecoach traffic around the taverns, and its colorful market place running westward along the High, or Market Street from the docks on the Delaware River. The shop windows were full of unsuspected treasures, and she loved to watch the late afternoon parade of high society along Chestnut Street. The Philadelphia society ladies were turned out by expensive dressmakers, milliners, and hairdressers in the latest imported styles from France and England. Everyone frequented the circulating library, available to all who cared to read, and used as a sort of club by its membership of "bluestockings," as the educated literary ladies were called, and their more or less learned beaux.

Many of the streets between the substantial brick buildings were paved, and were lighted at night, and a watchman patrolled with a lantern, calling out the hours between dusk and dawn. Narrow footways ran between the house fronts and the road, edged with stout wooden posts to protect the pedestrians from the carriage traffic. These posts were topped with the oil lamps which were lighted at dusk. Wooden pumps were placed at intervals along the footways, each one serving several households. The servants came to these to draw the daily supply of water, and carried it home in buckets and pitchers.

Philadelphia owed much of its comforts and orderliness to the quiet genius of its foremost citizen, Dr. Benjamin Franklin, who had organized a street-cleaning system and a fire-fighting company. He had also devised a smokeless stove which burned either coal or wood, and he provided his fellow citizens for years with amusement and instruction in his *Poor Richard's Almanac*. In 1783 when the Paynes arrived he was still representing his country in France, where he had joined the Peace Commission. His return home two years later at the age of seventy-nine was the occasion of welcoming ceremonies which must have been witnessed with excitement by the Payne children.

Dolley enjoyed sitting out on the front stoop as their neighbors did in the summer evenings. The humid riverside heat was reflected and retained by the narrow city streets and alleys and was often hard to bear, for one accustomed to the open air around Scotchtown. Through Nancy and Sally Drinker, Dolley and her brothers were soon members of the young Quaker society who contrived such innocent amusements as picnics, fishing, berrying, and skating parties—and small excursions to the outskirts of the city when the mail coach travelling through was willing to carry them no farther than they could walk back. They were not, of course, supposed to enter any of the many taverns along the road, as the best of these might be patronized by rather rough company. They carried their own homemade lunches in baskets to eat while they rested by the roadside.

Dolley's tall, slight figure, blue eyes, and brilliant complexion—always protected from the sun as her only jewel—soon attracted a string of suitors, who remained as much enthralled by her sunny nature and undesigning charm as by her beauty. By the time she was eighteen one of them, a serious young Quaker bachelor named John Todd, had become very faithful in his attentions, and was cheerfully regarded by all the other girls as Dolley's property. But in an age when girls usually either married in their teens or were considered old maids with something lacking, perverse Dolley Payne held out against custom and opinion and was even heard to say that she never meant to marry at all. Her gay young associates, marrying right and left themselves, began to wonder what she was waiting for.

The Quakers were rather gay, in the 1780s in Philadelphia, especially the "wet" Quakers, so called for the limpness of their principles. Some of them had deliberately relaxed the rules of dress and behavior so far as to wear hooped gowns, silks, colors, and jewelry. A few of them committed the utmost offense of marrying "out of Meeting"— outside the membership of the Society of Friends. This was a sin which shamed or sometimes estranged their families, as the culprit was publicly scolded and "read out of Meeting"— denied the right henceforth to join the silent, soul-searching congregation to worship in the Quaker way. Dolley had heard with awe the relentless words which banished some reckless acquaintance, to remain an outcast unless he or she was able to "convince" the new marriage partner and induce him to become a Quaker too. The early days of many a marriage must have been overshadowed by a sense of guilt and obligation thus imposed, and many an unhappy quarrel may have been started as a result.

In spite of her determined spinsterhood, Dolley revealed in a letter a secret sympathy for these romantic unions "contrary to the Discipline." "A charming little girl of my acquaintance, and a Quaker too, ran off and was married to a Roman Catholic the other evening," she wrote to a recent visitor to her home. "Thee may have seen her, Sally Bartram was her name. Betsy Wistar and Kitty Morris, two plain [Quaker] girls, have left to effect a union with the choice of their hearts; so thee sees Love is no respector of persons."

While Dolley grew in beauty and popularity in her new circle, her father's affairs became hopelessly entangled in debt and legal trouble arising out of his total ignorance of competitive business. The remains of the family capital from the sale of Scotchtown disappeared entirely. Much of the wealth of Philadelphia had always been in Quaker hands, and they had even been bitterly likened to the Jews for commercial genius, but John Payne had not the knack of making money. And a Quaker was at least expected always to be able to pay his own bills.

Humiliated and defeated in his bleak attempt to interpret and obey the "Inner Light" which he believed had led him to Philadelphia, he shut himself away from human society, remained for days behind the closed door of his bedroom, and finally took to his bed entirely, with what had become a nervous breakdown. Drowned in his own despair, tormented day and night by the apparent loss of communication with the Spirit which could reveal to him God's Will and wordlessly light his way through the world, he simply withdrew himself and waited for death to release him from the responsibilities which now fell upon his wife's shoulders.

Fortunately for all concerned, it was just about this time, in the spring of 1787, that a new convention began to assemble in the already hallowed chambers of the State House at Philadelphia, which eleven years before had seen the signing of the Declaration of Independence. Its members would be looking for places to dine and lodge, cleaner and quieter places than the old Indian Queen Tavern and Oeller's Hotel. Quaker food was always famous. Using Amy's little legacy to provide, Mary Payne opened the ground floor of her house on 3rd Street to gentleman boarders, who were received as members of the family.

2

First Marriage

Distracted as she was by the public distress of her family, Dolley at nineteen must have realized to some extent the importance of the convention which met at Philadelphia that summer.

The stormy decade between the Declaration of Independence and the Philadelphia Convention of 1787 had been a perilous experiment which, after a good beginning, now seemed about to fail. The Revolutionary War had been won, by a hair's breadth, through the heroic efforts of men who had gathered from every corner of the American colonies to defend their liberties. It was a ragged, dogged army under Washington's leadership which had at last seen the defeated British troops lay down their arms in the surrender field at Yorktown in 1781. Since then, under the Articles of Confederation hastily drawn up during the war emergency, the thirteen separate states had attempted to govern themselves without the King's authority or administrative machinery—without, it proved, any real authority at all, for there was no central government except the divided, ill-attended Congress sitting in New York City.

There the representatives of the thirteen triumphant colonies which had won the right to call themselves states bickered and bargained among themselves, each striving for a little more than equality among the others, while refusing to pay an equal share of the war debt or to accept equal taxation. Now the Treasury was empty—as it had been most of the time during the war. The North objected to the South and its slave economy. The South disputed the right of the North to criticize the way it chose to live, and pointed out that northerners had long indulged in the slave trade. The Middle States sided either way, or took their own line. Tensions rose, disunion grew, secession was openly talked of. There was no money in the Treasury to pay any sort of national police force to preserve a general peace amongst them. The very idea of nationhood was threatened, for there was no way to enforce cooperation.

Inevitably they turned back to the man who had brought them through the desperate war they had barely won— George Washington, now retired to his beloved acres on the Potomac, planting his trees, landscaping his grounds, laying out his gardens, and striving to raise on his impoverished soil the paying crops which could support his numerous dependents. Washington thought when he resigned his army commission in 1783 that he had laid down forever his responsibilities for the infant country he had fought to free. He was more than willing that younger and more ambitious men should carry it on from there—men like Alexander Hamilton, James Monroe, and that grave young lawyer from the Blue Ridge country, James Madison. But they would not leave him alone. Even his contemporaries, like John Adams, Thomas Jefferson, George Mason, Henry Knox, men who like himself had earned a peaceful old age, urged him to take the helm again. They placed themselves at his service, arguing that he was the only one among them who was capable of preserving as a united whole the thirteen widely differing states which had joined together under his leadership to throw off the British rule and set themselves up as an independent nation.

England was waiting to see them fail. France was watching the republican experiment in America with jealous, skeptical eyes. And Massachusetts, rebelling against its own tax system and the decisions of its local courts, was on the brink of civil war. In desperation the Congress at New York called for a convention of all the states to discuss the situation and find the remedy.

Delegates were named as in 1774 and 1775—often the same ones—to assemble at Philadelphia again. This time they must try to rewrite the loose Articles of Confederation and devise a form of government which would unite the many local factions and dissenting state legislatures, before the American states broke up into thirteen hostile communities at war among themselves which any European power would be able this time to conquer and annex.

Amongst the men who travelled the familiar road to Philadelphia in 1787 were some who held obstinately to the belief that each of the thirteen should be a sovereign state accountable only to its own inhabitants and legislature. Others, who would fortunately prevail, were convinced that each state must concede, that a compromise must be found for all, and that all must acknowledge a single, elected authority whose policies and decisions would be binding upon all. It can be seen that the seeds of further dispute and debate were already sown before the 1787 Convention ever assembled.

On Sunday, May 13, amidst a great chiming of bells and firing of salutes and cheers from the roadside, Washington arrived. Although he had intended in his modest way to lodge at the Market Street boarding house which had been a center for Virginian activities since the first Convention in 1774, he was at once carried off by his wealthy friend Robert Morris, to be a guest at the Morris mansion a few doors away.

As soon as enough delegates finally assembled, they got down to business and elected Washington as chairman, or president of the Convention. It was at once decided that absolute secrecy should be maintained—that nothing spoken in the House chamber should reach the outside world. The proceedings in the State House therefore went forward in the utmost privacy, the members being forbidden to discuss each day's developments in correspondence with their families or friends, much less in the coffee houses where they gathered to relax at the end of each day's work. Nothing was available at firsthand to the people who wrote for the few newspapers then in existence, though rumors were plentiful. Even Washington's daily entries in his brief Diary were discreetly bare of anything said or done within the chamber where he presided every day. Except for some painstaking notes jotted down during the often heated debates and forbidden publication until the middle of the following century, we would have no knowledge whatever of the rocky road which finally led to the Constitution of the United States as it stands today. Those priceless notes were taken by the small, fastidiously dressed, very articulate Virginia lawyer named James Madison.

He was thirty-six years old. In 1772 he had graduated from Princeton University in such poor health that he was believed doomed to an early death. He had since served on Committees of Correspondence and in the Virginia legislature and in Congress, but never in the army during the war because of his delicate physical condition. Unlike most of his Virginia colleagues, he was not a Tidewater man, but had grown up at Montpellier, his father's vast estate in the Blue Ridge foothills region called the Piedmont. His experience in the Congress had helped him to conquer a natural rural timidity arising from his secluded life and a lack of physical height and health in a lusty masculine time, but he had had scant opportunity to learn social accomplishments. His growing self-confidence was then destroyed by an unfortunate love affair with the daughter of a New York congressman named Floyd, who with his family was living at the same boarding house. Congressman Floyd had encouraged Madison's courtship of his daughter, and even Thomas Jefferson had approved the match. But Madison had too few drawing-room arts to attract young females, and after the engagement had been announced the heartless Miss Floyd jilted him for a young divinity student who was better able to appreciate and assist her performance on the harpsichord.

Jefferson, nearly ten years older than Madison and recently a widower, wrote a fatherly letter of advice and consolation to his protégé, who had retreated to Montpellier to lick his wounds. "I sincerely lament the misadventure which has happened, from whatever cause it may have happened. Should it be final, however, the world still presents the same and many other sources of happiness, and you possess many within yourself. Firmness of mind and unremitting occupation will not long leave you in pain."

Madison had gathered himself together and was again with the Congress in New York when the call to the Philadelphia Convention came. He had already worked out in his own mind a form of solution to the government's difficulties, and had prepared himself to present it to the Convention. He arrived at Philadelphia well in advance of the other delegates and took a room at the house where Washington would have stayed, were it not for Morris's hospitality. The unfortunate episode with Miss Floyd had taken its proper place in his perspective as over and done with, and he most sensibly intended to devote his whole mind and energies to the problem confronting them all.

Having witnessed the indecisions and quarrels of the old Congress at New York, he was very much aware of the need for improvement in the governing system. Perhaps even more clearly than anyone else, he saw the necessity to scrap the Articles of Confederation and base a new Constitution on the idea of a strong federal government which placed the welfare of the nation above state sovereignty, and gave the central government the power to enforce its collective will upon any dissenting unit.

He had already outlined this conviction to Washington at Mount Vernon and to his friend Edmund Randolph, who was governor of Virginia. Thomas Jefferson was now in France, acting as minister there since Dr. Franklin's return home. John Adams was in London as minister to the Court of St. James. Madison may have felt that they could manage just as well without Adams, as Massachusetts was already a problem. But he needed Washington and Randolph to back him up against the States Rights people, and those two were at hand. Also, as president of Pennsylvania at eighty-one, there was still Benjamin Franklin, receiving his visitors under the spreading mulberry tree in his garden.

Dolley Payne must often have stood among the respectful crowds which gathered round the entrance of the State House to watch the delegates pass in and out in the summer sunshine, as they had done back in 1774 before the Revolutionary War had begun in earnest. She would have seen Washington among them, for the first time, and surrounding him many of the famous and distinguished men she never thought to know personally—including the slight, dark-clad Virginia lawyer she was to marry only seven years later.

Meanwhile there was still John Todd, waiting faithfully for her to make up her mind. He had a substantial income from his law practice. He was Quaker bred, and their families both approved. But still Dolley hesitated, no one knew why, perhaps least of all herself.

Five hours a day, six days a week, the Convention was locked in debate as the struggle for power went on behind closed doors—States Rights or a strong central government. Tempers flared and were resolutely brought under control again. Washington sat impassive, patient, mostly in silence, while his colleagues wrangled. James Madison was present every day, sick or well, though the heat was oppressive to his mountain lungs. He spoke often and with obstinate adherence to his basic idea of Union, all for one, one for all. While making his closely reasoned speeches he sometimes seemed in his natural diffidence to address the inside of his hat, which he held before him in his hand and where perhaps brief notes were concealed. He was tireless in his defense of what became known as the Virginia Plan—which meant that he was urging the drafting of a whole new constitution for the United States, instead of an attempt to patch up the Articles of Confederation which had proved inadequate.

The Virginia Plan included the establishment of a national Treasury into which every state paid its taxes, a national Congress of two Houses, Senate and Representatives, and a single chief executive elected to serve seven years and to be ineligible for a second term. This last was later modified to four years, with the possibility of re-election. From the beginning there could be no doubt about the choice for the first president. Although he hoped that he might escape this further obligation, Washington was known to favor the Virginia or Federal Plan as the basis for a new government. The "bitter-enders" who opposed it held out stubbornly for the sovereign rights of each individual state, and muttered about the danger of monarchy.

When the Convention finally dispersed in September a document had been achieved, but by no means unanimously. A long and bitter fight for its ratification by each separate state convention awaited each delegate on his return home. Madison argued passionately at the Virginia Convention in Richmond in defense of his beliefs, against his friends Edmund Randolph and James Monroe, and such eloquent elder statesmen as Patrick Henry, who was supported by Washington's old friend George Mason. During this crucial time Thomas Jefferson and John Adams were still abroad on their ministerial duties in France and England.

It was 1789 before the Constitution was adopted and the new government was established in New York and functioning along the lines of Madison's original vision of Union. The first chief executive, to be called the president, was inaugurated in New York in April of that year. He began his administration in a rented house on Cherry Street, which soon proved too small and inconvenient for the purpose. There arose the question of a permanent location for the nation's capital and the residence of the governing body and the President.

It might seem that a suitable location could have been found or made in New York City or in what was then the center of civilization in the New World—Philadelphia. Instead, for a variety of complicated reasons, a site for the new capital was chosen on the Potomac River, almost midway between the North and South. There, on land ceded by the plantation owners of Virginia and Maryland, a whole new city would be erected with named and numbered streets laid out in a preconceived pattern, on what had been marshy pastures and hilly cornfields. French architects were hired to design and construct government buildings and a president's mansion. Speculation in building lots was lively, for land values were expected to soar in what was known in the beginning as the Federal City. Soon its name became simply Washington, in the District of Columbia.

In January of 1790 Dolley submitted to her invalid father's desire to see at least one of his family provided for before he died, and to John Todd's stubborn devotion. At the age of twenty-one she married the young Quaker lawyer who was seven years her senior. There is no evidence that she had changed her mind about her reluctance to marry at all, and she may have acted merely in obedience to the wishes of her elders, as most girls did in those days. Neither is there any reason to suppose that she was unhappy in what seemed to be her logical destiny as the dutiful wife of a suitable husband.

The Quaker marriage ceremony was as austere as all their other customs. The two young people stood up alone in Meeting, and a simple vow was spoken: "I, John Todd, take thee, Dolley Payne, to be my wedded wife and promise with divine assistance to be unto thee a loving and faithful husband until death shall separate us." Dolley spoke her vow after him, her hand in his. A long list of distinguished witnesses from Philadelphia's first Quaker families signed the marriage register, proving the high regard in which the Paynes and the Todds were held in that society.

There is no mention of Dolley's wedding dress, which may have been made of silk, but in a sober color without adornments. Somehow the impoverished Paynes provided the usual wedding supper for a number of guests, at which there was of course no music or dancing, and perhaps not much laughter. Although there were no bridesmaids or groomsmen according to the customs of other faiths, their closest attendants were Dolley's friends Eliza Collins and Anthony Morris (not related to the famous Morrises, Robert or Gouverneur). Both Eliza and Morris would be devoted to Dolley all her life, though both were soon to establish families of their own.

The young Todds began housekeeping in a rented house on Chestnut Street, with John's law office in the front room of the ground floor, as was customary. The rest of the house was comfortably furnished with mahogany and pine in designs which nowadays would have great distinction—carpets, mirrors, and other luxuries somewhat strained the Quaker rule of stark simplicity and sanded floors. Within a year they were able to move to a better house on 4th Street, which had a stable attached, and John bought a horse and a "riding-chair," which was a simple open carriage. It was in this house that Dolley's first child, a son they called Payne, was born early in 1792.

There were other signs that John Todd's long-awaited happiness caused him further to relax the Quaker Discipline, to indulge himself and his wife in worldly vanities. A portrait of her, painted by James Peale soon after her marriage, shows an open-necked dress with a folded lacy kerchief fastened by a handsome brooch framing the throat, and around her neck a four-strand gold chain necklace. The Quaker headdress for a married woman was modified into a fetching lace-edged cap with a lace band passing under the chin. Her hair, instead of lying in the smooth Quaker bands from a center parting, apparently had a natural wave and was cut in a fringe across her forehead. It is noticeable that in all the portraits of Dolley, from this first one to those painted in her old age, the artists always drew the corners of her mouth with a definite upward tilt—not quite a smile, but cheerful and happy.

Philadelphia was now enlivened by the arrival of the Congress from New York, which intended to reside there while the Federal City was being built on the Potomac. Congress took up its sessions in the familiar chambers of the State

House, and President Washington moved into the Morris mansion on Market Street where he had often been a guest. Now he had rented it from his friend Robert Morris, who in order to accommodate the president moved his family into a smaller house nearby. Washington's household was a numerous one, and included his wife's two grandchildren, Nelly Custis and her brother George Washington Parke Custis (known in the family as Washy), besides the usual staff of maids, secretaries, and aides.

With the serene, commanding figure of Washington at the helm again, and in time of peace, it seemed as though all would be well at last, and the Philadelphia hostesses surpassed themselves with balls and dinner parties, and all attended the formal entertainments in the presidential mansion. Jefferson returned from four years abroad as minister to France, and became secretary of state. The feud soon began between him and cocky young Alexander Hamilton, who was secretary of the treasury, then considered the highest office below the president. Edmund Randolph was named attorney general. John Adams, whose somewhat pompous ego had to be satisfied with the vice-presidency, was by nature a Federalist, which meant that he believed like Hamilton in a privileged governing class wielding the power of a strong central government. Adams brought his sharp-tongued Yankee wife Abigail to live in a large suburban house called Bush Hill, and neither of them was able to hide or control their jealousy of Washington's unassailable position as the most distinguished and popular man in the country.

Old John Payne had lived to see the first of his grandsons, Payne Todd, but he died a broken, defeated man, resigned against bitterness by his faith, though long rejected according to its austere standards. He left what little property he still possessed to his wife. The following summer of 1793 Dolley's younger sister Lucy, aged fifteen, made the most of the widely loosening Discipline and eloped with the president's nephew, George Steptoe Washington, son of Samuel. After a somewhat irresponsible boyhood, when he and his brother Lawrence had often put a severe strain on Washington's patience and purse, George Steptoe had recently been apprenticed at law in the office of the attorney general.

This time it was her own sister whom Dolley heard read out of Meeting while she sat, pregnant with her second child, beside her own Quaker husband, and the cold, hard words of the creed banished Lucy forever from the fold: "Whereas Lucy Payne . . . was educated in the profession of us the people call Quakers, but for want of living agreeable to the principles of Truth hath suffered herself to be joined in marriage to a man of a different persuasion from us in matters of Faith, by an hireling Priest, contrary to the known Rules of our Discipline, therefore we think it our duty . . . publicly to disown the said Lucy from being a member of our Society, until she give satisfaction for her outgoing. . . ."

Lucy never brought George Steptoe into the Quaker Faith as she had been enjoined to do for her own sake, but she did succeed in sobering him up to a surprising degree, considering his previous record. The young couple left the frivolities and extravagances of Philadelphia and retired to live on his neglected family estate, Harewood, in the Shenandoah country in what is now West Virginia. Samuel Washington had never been able to make Harewood pay, being an indolent man with none of his brother George's virtues. The young Washingtons applied themselves to its rehabilitation with some success, and Harewood was soon famous for its hospitality and cordial good spirits.

3

Death Comes
to Philadelphia

Philadelphia was both grand and gay as the year 1793 began, and its streets were crowded with fine carriages. Among these was the conspicuous cream-colored coach with painted panels drawn by four white horses and attended by postillions in scarlet and white livery, which was President Washington's official equipage. The wealthy Quaker families outdid each other in the display, so long forbidden by the Discipline to which many of them no longer submitted, of imported silks and satins and jewelry, worn even by the men. The Mifflins, Logans, Biddles, Morrises, and Lloyds were indistinguishable now by their dress and behavior from the old non-Quaker aristocracy of the Chews, Willings, and Shippens. Everyone enjoyed the concerts and the theater and the dancing assemblies and dinner parties which were also attended by their new guests, the French refugees from the Reign of Terror which followed Louis XVI's death on the scaffold in January.

Then, in midsummer, Death came to Philadelphia.

It began with the sudden mysterious illness of an obscure

man in Vine Street, who died of the same type of "bilious fever" which Dr. Benjamin Rush had already encountered in several other patients, who had recovered after being bled and purged. When more and more people died after showing the same symptoms, Rush realized that the city was falling into an epidemic which was apparently contagious. Tracing back, he found that most of the persons afflicted had been in the vicinity of the wharves before falling ill. It seemed to him that the fever spread by infection from the riverfront, where debris from the boat cargoes was often allowed to rot under the hot sun. Very soon Rush unwillingly identified the disease as the dread yellow fever from the tropics, perhaps carried by other refugees who were fleeing from a slave rebellion in the West Indies.

His wife was on a visit to Princeton, and he wrote her to stay there till he could advise her further. Influenza was also present in Philadelphia in a most violent form, and Rush was kept on the go day and night attending his many patients and hundreds more who begged for his assistance by crowding round outside the door of his house in Walnut Street. He was a conscientious doctor with what was in those days a real gift for healing. Moreover, he was always deeply interested in the cause and origin of the diseases he was called upon to treat. Often his conclusions and theories were ridiculed by other physicians, and numerous quacks flourished in what was then still the dark ages of medicine.

But as the fatal fever spread throughout the city, westward from the riverfront, desperate remedies were resorted to in the hope of stopping the infection. In case it was carried by dust due to the unusual drought, the fire companies were advised to wet down the streets at frequent intervals. As people became familiar with the early warning signs, which were common to many more minor illnesses—headache, nausea, giddiness, sore throat, and sweating—panic sent them scurrying to the already overworked doctors or caused them to crawl into bed to await the worst. The crisis of the ailment was often passed in five days, when the patient either died or made a slow and painful recovery.

The Pennsylvania College of Physicians issued a list of precautions which was published in the newspapers—avoid infected persons and houses, quarantine the houses where the sickness had appeared, clean up the streets and wharves where odorous waste accumulated. But the frightened populace was preparing to flee the city streets for lodgings in the countryside, where they would find a cool reception and often be refused entrance at inns and farms which had hitherto been glad to let rooms for the summer holidays. City houses were closed up entirely, or left to the care of resentful servants who only wanted to be taken along with the family to whatever protection the suburban air provided.

By early September, Philadelphia looked like a city awaiting the onslaught of an invading army, as scores of families loaded their household belongings into carts, wagons, even wheelbarrows and gypsy bundles, and set out on the hot dusty roads on foot or with whatever horses could be bought or hired for transport. Business came to a standstill. The bells which were customarily tolled for funerals were ordered stopped, to reduce the mounting terror of the death count. The sick were left untended in deserted houses, when even members of the same family fled in panic. The dead were left unburied, as fear of contact with corpses grew.

Dr. Rush sent his young sons to join their mother at Princeton lest they catch the infection from his clothes when he returned from his rounds among the sick and dying. The government moved to the suburb of Germantown, where Washington took a rented house for his family, and the Cabinet secured whatever cramped quarters were available in the immediate neighborhood.

An emergency hospital was established at Bush Hill, now deserted by the Adams family, and there some of the luckier ones among the stricken were cared for if they were 'abandoned or had no one to attend to their bare necessities. There was much dissension among the doctors as to the best treatment, but everything was tried in their desperation—purges, quinine (or bark, as it was called), herbs, brandy—even wrapping the patient in blankets dipped in warm vinegar, which was supposed to disinfect and stimulate—but still they died. Rush tried frequent bleeding, cold water baths, doses of rhubarb or calomel and jalap (made from powdered morningglory seeds), cooling liquids to drink, like barley-water and weak camomile tea. He prescribed only soft foods such as gruel, tapioca, wine whey, white chicken meat, and fruit. The floor and hangings of the sickrooms were liberally sprinkled with vinegar, which was supposed also to protect the volunteer attendants from the infection.

Rush's medical colleagues attacked his methods in favor of their own, and some of them left the city themselves to avoid the risk of contact with the disease. There were no longer any funeral processions, and the hearse and dead-carts were often unaccompanied, and grief "descended below weeping," so that one more death brought little show of emotion in the sorrow-stunned city. Black mourning clothes were given up because they only caused the wearer to be avoided as a possible source of contamination.

Through it all the lean, compassionate Dr. Rush came and went, himself unaffected except for a growing exhaustion, spending himself generously for rich and poor alike, and striving always to learn more about the affliction in order to discover its cause and cure. He noted that it attacked people of all ages, men more frequently than women, white people oftener than Negroes. People who shut up their homes, closing doors and windows in the pitiless heat, and avoided going out except to procure food sometimes escaped the infection altogether.

The lack of trained nurses and physicians in Philadelphia was certainly responsible for many deaths from want of care. The remaining doctors and nurses, many of them willing amateurs among whom were many Quakers, worked around the clock till they themselves dropped from exhaustion or the fever. Rush remained miraculously immune, though members of his own household, student assistants and servants, caught the disease and died under his hands. "I was favored," he wrote in a later account of those dreadful days, "with an exemption from the fear of death in proportion as I subdued every selfish feeling, and labored exclusively for the benefit of others."

When they were turned away from the crowded parlors of the few remaining doctors, or found the doors locked against them, the terror-stricken people devised their own preventives and remedies. Some believed that smoking tobacco warded off the infection, and even women and children kept a cigar constantly in their mouths. Others chewed garlic all day and carried it in their clothes. Others drenched everything with camphor or vinegar, or burned gunpowder or tar as disinfectant. A natural result of the general apprehension was to produce the giddiness, quickened pulse, or stomach disorders which might be regarded as warning signals of the fever. At the end of the summer, what with nervous tension, grief, and the inevitable hot weather complaints, Rush recorded that no one in the city was perfectly well.

With business at a standstill, food and money became scarce. The city was paralyzed with calamity, and houses in the surrounding countryside, flooded with refugees who often had made no provision to pay their unwilling hosts, began to bar their doors against destitute late-comers who might be carrying the infection to those who believed they had got away in time. The roadsides outside of town were strewn with hopeless families, surrounded by their few portable possessions, exhausted and homeless, with crying children and bewildered old folk, looking for any kind of shelter.

Finally in mid-September, Rush recognized in himself the unmistakable symptoms of the fever. He took his own remedies, bled himself, and went to bed. Within a few days he was up and about again, still very weak and unwell, but able to see patients in his parlor, and to make his house-to-house calls. In October he collapsed across the bed of a patient and was carried home, where he remained prostrate with chills and vomiting for two weeks, in the care of one of his students, before a slow improvement began.

Mrs. Payne's friend, Eliza Drinker, among other Quakers, apparently never left the city the whole summer, and she noted briefly in her diary the weekly mortality figures as they climbed to 750. "Seventeen graves were dug in the Friends' burying ground yesterday," she wrote in October. " 'Tis very affecting to walk through the streets of our once flourishing and happy city; the houses shut up from one corner to another, the inhabitants that remain keeping shut up—very few seen walking about.... The weather is much changed this evening; it blows hard from the N.W. and is very cold."

The cold spell she mentioned proved to be the turning point in the epidemic, and thereafter it was on the wane. By then the city orphanage was full of waifs whose parents had died of the plague or abandoned them in flight from it. Eliza Drinker was spared, and although Rush's purging and bloodletting were much criticized at the time and seem primitive by medical practice today, many of his patients recovered, especially if he reached them in the early stages. And certainly his selfless devotion to his profession deserves the highest praise, when some other doctors spared themselves, or fled from their responsibilities altogether.

Dolley Todd's second child had been born in August, just before the city dissolved into panic. But her prudent young husband conveyed her on a litter, with the two babies, to a house on the bank of the Schuylkill River outside the town, where her mother and sisters soon joined her. Without Todd's solicitude and prompt action, James Madison might never have had a wife named Dolley, and much of the luster of this country's early history might have been lost. John Todd himself returned to Philadelphia, where his aged parents preferred to remain, and where he felt he could be of some use.

He arrived there in time to prepare his father's will, written out on his deathbed. The old man left John £500, and bequeathed his silver watch to his eldest grandson Payne. Todd's mother died soon after, and he was detained by pleas from all sides for his legal assistance. Finally he felt in himself the ominous first symptoms, and regardless of possible contagion he rushed back to his family on the Schuylkill. Dolley ran to meet him at the threshold, where it is said he collapsed and died, happy to have seen her "once more."

In the autumn the refugees began to return from the country. Those citizens of Philadelphia who had lived through that dreadful summer—either by some mysterious immunity or by recovering from the fever—were confronted by the heart-breaking task of cleaning and fumigating the devastated city.

Many households burned bedding and clothing they feared had been infected. Walls and woodwork were scrubbed and whitewashed, and all rooms were thrown wide open, to the healing fresh air. Much thought was given to preventing a recurrence next year, and everything thought capable of harboring infection was destroyed.

Meetings of learned men and physicians endlessly debated the origin of the plague. Rush at first believed that it was contagious from person to person, but later changed his mind about that. It was another hundred years before a man named Walter Reed at the head of an army medical team proved on human volunteers his theory that yellow fever was transmitted by a certain species of mosquito and no other way. We know now, of course, that the first frosts killed the mosquitoes which bred in the many rain barrels and stagnant pools of dirty water and slime, but then Philadelphia was only relieved to find that the cool weather had brought relief.

By the time the first snow fell, the city was nearly normal again, though 10 per cent of its population had died, and Rush's courage and devotion to duty had become a legend. The government returned to the State House and its usual lodgings, the president was back in the Morris mansion with his wife and the Custis children. Business resumed briskly, and there began to be talk of another war with the British because of their highhanded interference with American shipping at sea. Lights shone again behind the windows of the houses, large and small. The theater reopened. People began to send out invitations to balls and dinner parties. Life renewed itself, with a little extra warmth of reunion, and thankfulness for the sight of familiar faces when so many were missing forever.

Whether from yellow fever or not, Dolley was dangerously ill after Todd's death at their country refuge. Their youngest child died, leaving her with one son who was nearly two years old when she returned with him to the house in Philadelphia where he had been born. Her mother and sisters had nursed her devotedly, and now she was a widow like her mother. Mary Payne was fifty, and Dolley Todd was not yet twenty-five.

Her inheritance from the Todd estate was enough to keep her in modest comfort in her own home which John Todd had provided. Soon her natural good spirits and happy nature asserted themselves, and she bloomed with such radiant beauty that people turned to look at her in the street.

It was hardly fitting that so young and attractive a widow should live alone, and her younger sister Anna, to whom she was always most closely attached, came to live with her. The youngest girl, Mary, remained with her mother for whom she was named, to assist in the reopening of the boarding house for congressmen which Mrs. Payne had maintained before her husband's death. Its reputation soon attracted back the usual clientele during the winter of 1793–94, and among them was the rather flashy young senator from New York, Aaron Burr.

4

"Dolley Madison! Alass! Alass!!"

It is likely that Burr was already acquainted with the Payne family and probably also with the young Todds, for society in those days was small and Quakers stood high in the estimation of all. Burr's own reputation had been tarnished with gossip which his self-confident air and bright roving eye did little to squelch. He had served for a brief time as one of Washington's officers at Headquarters, and was said to have earned the General's lasting displeasure by being caught in the act of reading private papers on Washington's desk. Promotion in the army came too slowly to suit him, though he was present at the battle of Monmouth, where he suffered a severe and disabling sunstroke in the terrible heat of the day.

He had married in 1782 a widow somewhat older than himself, at whose home in Hohokus many of the younger officers had found hospitality during the dreary New Jersey campaigns, and after the war he established his home and law practice in New York City. In 1784 he was elected to the New York Legislature, but was not a member of the Convention at

Philadelphia which drew up the Constitution. His wife's health had failed fast after the birth of their only child, Theodosia, and when Burr accompanied the new Congress to Philadelphia in the autumn of 1791 he left her and their daughter in a comfortable New York home.

By then the political lines had been drawn between the Federal and anti-Federal parties, and an enmity had already begun between Burr and Alexander Hamilton, both of them ambitious and rather ruthless young men. Burr was openly on the make, and in financial difficulties, whereas Hamilton had married the daughter of wealthy General Schuyler of New York State. Burr tried for the governorship of New York, and lost it to George Clinton. He wanted the appointment as minister to France, and James Monroe got that. He wanted to be chosen vice-president in the second Washington administration, and John Adams was re-elected to that.

Burr opposed Hamilton in every possible way, and was accused of courting the Madison-Jefferson partnership in his own interests. Washington stood apart, staunchly Federal in his belief in a strong central government as conceived by Madison. Jefferson's more radical Republican views were not yet much in evidence.

In May of 1794 Burr's wife died in New York during his absence. He found himself a widower at thirty-eight, with a daughter eleven years old, whose education he had always supervised with the most loving care. Although he was much away from home, he wrote Theodosia long, fatherly letters with minute instructions for her studies and behavior. After his wife's death he brought the child to Philadelphia, where she attended one of the excellent girls' schools in the city.

It was well known that Burr interested himself in a practical way with orphaned or destitute children—a side of his nature which was oddly at variance with his other reputation as a lady-killer and political opportunist, ready to sacrifice principle to advancement. He was anyway a trusted friend of Mrs. Payne and her younger children, and it was doubtless because of her mother's confidence in a man who had been a member of her household off and on for several years that Dolley Todd named him as the guardian of her baby son Payne. It has been supposed that Burr was attracted to Dolley even before the death of his wife released him to appear among the several eligible suitors for the young Quaker widow, and this may have been true, as he was never indifferent to a pretty woman. There is nothing to verify this assumption beyond her action with regard to Payne.

In any case, very little time elapsed between his wife's death, which was long expected, and an evening when at James Madison's request he brought his fellow congressman to call on Dolley at the 4th Street house. One of Dolley's earliest surviving letters sets the scene. Her girlhood friend Eliza Collins had recently married Richard Bland Lee, another congressman from Virginia. Eliza had consequently been disowned in Meeting—but in her new matronly status she was apparently considered a more suitable chaperon than young Anna Payne. In this year of 1794, Eliza received a somewhat flurried note from the beautiful widow Todd: "Dear Friend, thou must come to me—Aaron Burr says that the great little Madison has asked to be brought to see me this evening."

It is possible that she and Madison had already met at some more formal occasion, and that Madison wished to make further acquaintance with a woman he had perhaps admired from a respectful distance, and had asked the assistance of a mutual friend. Burr, with his supreme self-assurance, would hardly have expected anything to come of it, even if he had had himself any serious intentions towards Dolley then. Madison was "great," it was true, in the halls of Congress and in the estimation of Philadelphia society, but he was always shy with women, he dressed soberly, and cut no very impressive figure in a ballroom. If it had occurred to Burr to count up, Madison was then forty-three—seventeen years older than Dolley Todd, five years older than Burr.

No woman could have failed to be flattered and perhaps flustered by the prestige of the two callers Dolley received that evening, but her natural charm and gaiety of spirit would have warmed away any constraint with the polished, overconfident senator from New York and the less showy Virginian who was already known as the Father of the Constitution and who had by his eloquence and perseverance won its adoption against strong opposition in his native state.

The evening probably passed in light conversation expertly conducted, and was enlivened by delicious refreshments prepared by practiced Quaker hostesses. Dolley wore "a mulberry gown," with a filmy white kerchief folded in the neck, and a gauzy cap on her dark hair. Madison's usual handsome black was relieved by fine white lace at the throat and wrists, silver buckles on his shoes and at the knees above black silk stockings. Burr would have worn the more fashionable rich maroon, royal blue, or bottle-green which well-dressed gentlemen used then.

Madison soon appeared in 4th Street again, without the support of a companion—and again, till it became a courtship which was remarked on by all Philadelphia. There is a legend that through the Paynes' connection to the president's family by Lucy's marriage to George Steptoe Washington, Dolley Todd had become a welcome and informal visitor to the Washingtons in the Morris mansion only a few doors away. Because of her granddaughter Nelly Custis, Martha took a lively interest in the romantic attachments of the younger government set. In this way she heard of Madison's attentions to

Dolley, and is supposed to have expressed official approval of a match between one of the president's most favored young men and Lucy's sister.

When Madison's usual summer sojourn with his parents at Montpellier in Orange County fell due, Dolley set off in almost the opposite direction with her sister Anna and four-year-old Payne Todd and his nurse, to make a round of visits near her old home in the Tidewater country. Apparently when they parted she had not given a definite answer to a definite proposal of marriage from Madison. It was a little soon, for Dolley, and she wanted time to think. Only a year ago she and John Todd had fled from the city where yellow fever was raging. In the interim she had lost a husband and her younger child. She had adjusted to a new life in her own establishment with an income of her own. She was surrounded by an admiring circle of friends, among whom were several very eligible men who had probably already declared themselves—such as Anthony Morris, who had attended her wedding to Todd, and William Wilkins who acted as her attorney and was permitted a sort of brotherly relationship. Dolley had a choice. Besides, Madison was not a Quaker.

He wisely let her go away for her visits—even rode with her carriage for part of the way, and then turned westward towards Montpellier. He was no impetuous boy, to hurry her. He returned home, where his family ties were strong, to wait.

Lucy Washington's home, Harewood, was not an impossible distance from Montpellier, however, and Mrs. Payne had been persuaded to give up her Philadelphia house and take the younger children to live in Harewood's expansive hospitality. It seems likely that there was some arrangement between Madison and Dolley that she would end her tour there, and he would join her for a visit, perhaps to press for his answer in that happy household.

Midway of her trip Dolley fell ill in Hanover County, probably of malaria, and a French house guest at Montpellier who
could not speak English was stricken with a sudden severe
sickness. Madison as his only interpreter could not leave him.
Several despairing letters must have passed between Hanover
and Orange counties during early August, with their plans
gone awry. Perhaps Madison did better with his practiced pen
than face to face in her little parlor. Perhaps his quiet strength
and good sense and steady devotion began to outshine all
other, showier claims, as Dolley recovered her health and took
time to consider.

She was not at this time a very clever woman, or a very
experienced one. Certainly she had no ambition to enter high
society, and certainly there was no indication then that Madison would ever surpass a man like Burr on the political scene.
Her first marriage had not been based on any ardent youthful
romance, and she was now a matron of twenty-six. She wanted
love, to be sure, and cherishing, as any woman does, and a kind
companion with whom to live out her life. And so she chose
Madison.

She wrote him so, from Fredericksburg, where her journey
towards Harewood had been interrupted by fatigue after her
illness. His reply was delayed until a servant could be spared
from Montpellier to carry it to her. Her letter to him is lost.
His reply, part of which is missing, seems to have been almost
worn out with much rereading and refolding, and has been
carefully preserved. Its formal phrasing could not hide the
relief and exultation of the man who wrote it:

"Orange, August 18, 1794. I received some days ago your
precious favor from Fredericksburg. I cannot express, but
hope you will conceive the joy it gave me. The delay in hearing of your leaving Hanover, which I regard as the only satis-
factory proof of your recovery, has filled me with extreme

inquietude, and the confirmation of that welcome event was endeared to me by the style in which it was conveyed. I hope you will never have another deliberation on that subject. If the sentiments of my heart can guarantee those of yours, they assure me there can never be a cause for it."

They both arrived at Harewood in September, and Madison became more urgent. He was aware of his rivals in Philadelphia, and wanted to make sure that Dolley would return there as his wife, leaving no opportunity for some one to change her mind.

Harewood was delighted at the prospect of a wedding, and preparations went forward briskly. Guests began to arrive, including George Steptoe Washington's young sister Harriot, whose naive admiration of the bride won Dolley's heart forever. A Winchester clergyman distantly related to Madison was sent for to perform the ceremony—Dolley in her turn would be read out of Meeting in Philadelphia. The beautiful drawing-room of Harewood, panelled in Palladian style, with a fine mantelpiece, was decorated by the young ladies with autumn flowers and greenery, and after the formal proceedings had taken place a typical Virginia wedding party with almost riotous gaieties began. In contrast to Dolley's first wedding, there was music and dancing and feasting and hearty laughter, as more and more guests arrived by carriage and on horseback till the big house overflowed.

Oddly enough, there is no record of what Dolley wore to be married in, but Madison's beautiful Mechlin lace cravat made such an impression that it was snipped to bits to make souvenirs by the laughing girls who held him captive till their ruthless scissors had done their work. He bore it with good grace and his usual composure, but to so staid a bachelor it must have been a surprising introduction to Dolley's family circle.

During the morning before the ceremony Dolley "stole away from the company" to write to her dear friend Eliza Collins Lee, who had gone abroad with her husband. This curious letter reveals that, just as in her marriage to Todd, Dolley still had some reservations and second thoughts: "In the course of this day I give my hand to the man who of all others I most admire. You will not be at a loss to know who this is, as I have long ago been gratified in having your approbation. In this union I have everything that is soothing and grateful in prospect—and my little Payne will have a generous and tender protector. A settlement of all my real property with a considerable addition of money is made upon him with Mr. M's full approbation. This I know you feel an interest in, or I would not have troubled you with it. You are also acquainted with the unmerited censure of my enemies on the subject."

These mysterious "enemies" could only have been among her old Quaker friends who held firmly to the Discipline of marriage within the Faith, and felt that in Madison's Episcopal household Todd's child would not be brought up as his father would have wished.

In the years to come "my little Payne" proved to be almost the only unhappy association that his too indulgent mother ever encountered, and he was responsible for an endless drain on Madison's own finances and patience. Any misgivings she may have felt on what Madison always considered the "luckiest" day of his life were misplaced, but they appear again in an odd little postscript scribbled at the end of her letter to Eliza, perhaps with her new husband actually in the same room: "Evening—*Dolley Madison*! Alass! Alass!!" she wrote, and sealed it up.

5

Second President

Although Madison wrote his parents from Harewood to announce his marriage, which would have come as no surprise to them, the wedding journey did not include Montpellier. They went on the usual tour of visits as far as his married sister Nelly Hite's new house, Belle Grove near Winchester. There Dolley was overtaken by an apparent recurrence of the fever which had prostrated her in August. Fortunately, in the informal fashion of the times, her sister Anna and Harriot Washington had accompanied them on what might be called their honeymoon—and the girls were there to assist in nursing Dolley. Payne and his nurse had been left at Harewood with Lucy, and rejoined his mother after she reached Philadelphia. Madison had arranged to occupy the house in Spruce Street where his friend Monroe had lived until his recent departure for France to act as American minister to the chaotic Revolutionary government.

James Monroe was the third of the so-called Virginia musketeers, Jefferson, Madison, and Monroe. Like Burr, he had served briefly in the army during the war, before retiring to study law under Jefferson, who was then governor of Virginia. While a member of the Congress sitting in New York in 1786, Monroe had married a New York heiress named Eliza Kortwright, whose friends were of the opinion that she could have done much better than the rather raw-boned and enigmatic young Virginian of twenty-eight, who had very little money and whose prospects at that time were not brilliant.

Monroe soon left the Congress and took his wife to Fredericksburg, where he established a law practice, and where he remained while the Convention met at Philadelphia to form the Constitution. When he decided to return to politics he and Madison campaigned together during Jefferson's absence in France. Monroe won the senatorship, while Madison went into the House of Representatives in the first Congress under the new Constitution. Ambitious, as Madison was not, and by some people considered a little tricky, Monroe became one of the first professional politicians. He joined with Madison in the struggle for power against Hamilton, and he won the French diplomatic post from both Hamilton and Burr, after Madison had declined it. At the same time John Jay of New York was sent as envoy to Great Britain, which caused France to distrust the American administration.

Those were critical times in Europe. Robespierre had recently fallen from power to be replaced by the National Convention in Paris which placed Bonaparte in command of its army. The United States was treading a narrow and perilous path of neutrality between England and France, while negotiations for the control of the Mississippi and the lands west of it moved cautiously forward. Algerian pirates in the Mediterranean were another dangerous problem. Monroe's immediate partiality for the French clashed with Jay's fondness for the English, and he was the less experienced and adroit of the two diplomats.

Madison, who doubtless considered himself well out of it,

settled down in Philadelphia with a household composed of his bride, her sister Anna, and her small, spoilt son Payne Todd, with assorted domestics. He received sincere congratulations on his marriage from his friends, many of whom had some knowledge of the widow Todd and approved his choice. Jefferson wrote of his fears that Madison might be tempted to retire from politics into the happy domesticity of which Jefferson himself had been robbed by the death of his wife many years before. Dolley would doubtless have been quite content with such a future. Instead, she found herself pitched at once into the political vortex she called "public business." With her usual adaptability she set about learning to be a capable and popular hostess to her husband's friends and colleagues. Happily she had no political bias of her own, and never developed or expressed such a thing. She was ready to receive everyone with disarming cordiality, even the controversial French refugees who had poured into the country to escape the Terror in France.

Although George Washington had been secured for a second term as president, much against his wishes and Martha's, the new nation in America had begun to show signs of falling apart. Jefferson had retired as secretary of state and returned to his home at Monticello. He was succeeded by Edmund Randolph. The commercial treaty which John Jay concluded with England was regarded as an unsatisfactory compromise, and Hamilton's support of it and of Jay's partiality for England increased his own unpopularity. Somewhat to Madison's surprise, Washington supported Jay and Hamilton, and Monroe's course in France was so violently criticized at home that his recall was under consideration. Washington's main object at this time was of course to preserve his infant nation from a ruinous war with one or the other of the great European powers.

Released from the austerities of a Quaker household, Dolley's younger sister Anna, who was about twenty at this time, became something of a belle in Philadelphia society. She was a popular partner at the brilliant Philadelphia dancing assemblies, which were held in the sixty-foot ballroom of Oeller's Hotel, a splendid room which had a musicians' gallery at one end and French wallpaper.

Beneath the frivolous front in Philadelphia lay the dark, disturbing facts of the French Revolution and the coming election of a second president of the United States, for Washington's retirement in 1797 was known to be inevitable.

Two political parties were formed during the last years of his administration—the Federalist, believing in a strong central government, a privileged class designed to govern, formal etiquette and distinguished good manners; and the so-called Democratic or "Republican" party which sympathized with the spirit of the French Revolution even while deploring its excesses, and hoped for a general leveling of society. Washington stood for the former in his stately appearance and strict adherence to the dignities of the presidency, and he insisted on United States neutrality in European affairs. Unfortunately the snobbery and ambition of Alexander Hamilton, and the unpopularity of John Jay since his treaty with Great Britain, were also attached to the Federalist side, as was the somewhat pompous John Adams, who could not stomach young Hamilton's arrogant ways. Jefferson, having left France before the Terror began, was the chief representative of the Republican spirit in America, though he had apparently retired from politics and was living at Monticello in Virginia. Madison maintained friendship with both Washington and Jefferson, and "Madisonians" was the term applied by his opponents to the men who like him held to the original constitutional intent, as set forth in that document ten years before.

A mild form of rivalry arose between him and Jefferson, as they tried to convince each other that the *other* one should be the next president, after Washington's second term expired. It was an idea which appealed even less to Madison than to Jefferson, for besides the Virginia planter's love of his own acres, he was devoted to his aging parents and younger brothers and sisters at Montpellier. Madison always insisted on the double *l* in the name of his home, and called the omission of the second *l* "a Yankee trick played on the French language."

Madison had paid a brief visit home with Dolley in the spring and summer of 1795, to introduce her to his family circle, where everyone fell in love with her at once. Alterations to the house were begun at that time to enlarge it sufficiently to accommodate the two families they had now become, as Dolley's little son and her sister Anna were always with her. Returning to Philadelphia in the autumn, they ran into the controversy over Jay's unpopular treaty with England, a document which appeared to sacrifice American interests to British influence for the sake of Britain's good will, but Madison refused to remonstrate against Washington's unwilling acceptance of it. At the same time the Cabinet was shaken by rumors of secret negotiations between Edmund Randolph as secretary of state and the French Minister Fauchet, which resulted in Randolph's enforced resignation.

The Madisons spent the summer at Montpellier again the next year, overseeing the enlargement of the house which gave the senior Madisons their own apartments. Madison also busied himself with introducing rotation of crops and fertilization of the exhausted land. He was becoming more and more interested in experimental farming, and began to think seriously of retiring from politics in order to live at home with Dolley, who was more than willing to forego the gaieties of Philadelphia life for the spacious quiet of Montpellier. At the same time he refused the governorship of Virginia, which was offered to him unanimously.

He did return to Philadelphia unwillingly in November, to encounter the election turmoil which was then beginning. The third presidential election in the United States was the first to be actually contested, after Washington's firm intention to retire in 1797 without a third term became plain to all. By the provisions of the Constitution then, the president was to be elected by a complicated system of electors chosen in each state, either by its legislature or by popular vote, as the state preferred, and composing what was called the Electoral College. Each elector would then cast his vote for two men, and the one with the most votes would be proclaimed president. The loser, with the second highest number of votes, was to be vice-president, preside over the Senate, and succeed the president in the event of his death or incapacity. The votes of the electors would be sent to the Senate to be counted and announced.

It can be seen that a reckless or contrived scattering of votes between the two top men could easily upset the majority, and possibly cause a tie or even a reversal of the overall intention. It is also obvious that the framers of the Constitution made little allowance for the popular preference of the country at large, or for the personal feelings of the defeated candidate, who was expected to work in harmony thereafter with the victor.

So long as Washington was available, there was never any doubt about who should be president, but the contest for second place had begun with his second term, when Adams won the vice-presidency for the second time, over George Clinton of New York. Jefferson had then received 4 votes, and Aaron Burr 1.

With Washington's final retirement in 1797, real confusion

began. Adams, after two vice-presidencies, seemed the logical successor to the presidency. But Hamilton was now his enemy, and Jefferson was his popular rival as the choice of the Republican or anti-Federal party. Hamilton above all detested Jefferson's Republican beliefs, and produced his own Federalist candidate, Charles Coatsworth Pinckney of South Carolina. Burr, who was then a member of the New York legislature at Albany, was also in the running as an anti-Hamilton Federalist.

Madison wrote to Jefferson at Monticello, urging him for the sake of the country to reconcile himself to accepting second place under Adams, failing first place, if the ballots went that way, and expressing the hope that the old friendship between Jefferson and Adams would always be maintained against the Hamilton influence.

Neither Adams nor Jefferson showed any interest in the campaign. Adams remained in his library at Braintree in Massachusetts; Jefferson was absorbed in his agricultural experiments in Virginia. They issued no "platforms," made no speeches or promises, and put nothing in writing even to their intimates. Nevertheless the campaign opened without them and was fought for them by their respective supporters. Jefferson was accused of everything from atheism to condoning the savagery of the French Revolution, which was not the way American freedom had been won. Adams was dubbed "His Rotundity" by the Republicans, in mockery of his alleged respect for titles, and it was predicted that he would only continue the errors of Washington's administration, which would surely result in a war with France. Hamilton intrigued tirelessly against Jefferson, whom he feared, and against Burr, whom he hated. Even the refugee foreigners joined in, reviling the Jay Treaty on one hand and the French Directory on the other. Jefferson wrote to Adams privately that their "personal feelings" towards each other need not be affected by the oratory of their respective supporters, and added that he had no desire for "a painful and thankless office." Adams wrote back pathetically of "treacherous friends and open enemies."

It was the official duty of the vice-president as president of the Senate to proclaim the results of the Electoral College ballot, which read: Adams 71, Jefferson 68, Pinckney 59, Burr 30. Jefferson had escaped the presidency by three votes, but his happy retirement at Monticello was at an end. As the second man on the ballot, he had to be vice-president.

Adams's inauguration on March 4, 1797, was a moving scene, as the realization struck the whole country that Washington, to whom they had held fast despite all the criticism of him by the politicians and foreigners—Washington was leaving them. The new president, in his neat gray suit, purposely plain and unostentatious, was completely overshadowed by the tall, self-possessed figure in black velvet who stood bowing his silent farewell to the tearful crowd which had gathered in the street outside the State House. Madison and Dolley were there, and it was to be her last sight of the first president, who would die of a sudden fatal cold at Mount Vernon before Adams had completed three years in office.

6

Third President

Madison considered that Washington's retirement to Mount Vernon justified his own return to Montpellier, and with Dolley he made a leisurely homeward journey in that spring of 1797, accompanied by Anna, little Payne, and Madison's sister Fanny, who had been in Philadelphia on a visit. It was his intention finally to leave the political scene for a quiet life of farming and study and domesticity with the wife he adored, while Adams coped with the country's problems as best he could. Many doubts and questions clouded the political air. Bonaparte's brilliant rise to power in France was not the least of these, though it seemed to promise some sort of order in Europe. Madison refused to take part in a proposed United States Mission to France, though the appointment was urged by Hamilton, and consequently opposed by some of the other Federalists.

During an interchange of visits between Montpellier and Monticello in the ensuing months, the friendly conversations and arguments ranged from the dangerous international triangle of France, England, and the United States, to various fascinating agricultural matters such as crop rotation and fertilizers, and the rebuilding of Montpellier which still continued and reflected Jefferson's devotion to classical architecture. Monroe, still smarting from his experience as minister to France, was also engaged in building a house, on a site near Monticello which had been chosen for him by Jefferson and Madison.

When the government reassembled in the autumn of 1797, Jefferson was of course compelled to go to Philadelphia for the vice-presidency, from where he wrote with discretion to his two friends in Virginia, believing that his mail was tampered with and read en route. Adams's Cabinet was full of intrigue and dissension, of which he was only half aware. Hamilton, who had served on Washington's staff during the Revolution, was now ready to go to war with France over the Mississippi lands and free navigation of the river, but he was demanding seniority of rank over General Henry Knox, who had fought from Boston to Yorktown with distinction.

Adams, a conceited man, was disgruntled at the closeness of the vote, and the 1796 election had resulted in the unhappy combination of a Federalist president and a Republican vice-president. The Cabinet was Federalist, though divided in allegiance between Adams and Hamilton. Jefferson felt his position as an accident of the electoral system, and made himself inconspicuous on the Philadelphia scene, where society remained largely Federalist in tone. People had reacted violently against the Terror and the guillotine in France, which Jefferson had appeared to condone in the name of liberty and equality for all. England still stood for monarchy and despotism in the eyes of his Republican followers, and Hamilton's policy was friendship with England at almost any cost. Both European nations were inclined to bully the United States, and Adams was determined, as Washington had been, to avoid war with either, which were already at war with each other.

Jefferson, who disapproved of the course of events in every possible way, took almost no part in the administration and was never consulted by Adams through a stormy four years, while the party spirit grew more and more inflamed, and Hamilton thrived on the strife he encouraged. Jefferson enjoyed the presidency of the Philosophical Society, which brought him the intellectual companionship he craved, and imposed no demands on him outside his own quiet circle.

Government policies became so unpopular with the opposition that there were finally rumors in the South of a movement to secede from the Adams regime. This was a prospect of disaster which dragged Madison out of a bout of dysentery and sent him down to the legislature at Richmond, of which he was a member. His friend, and Jefferson's, James Monroe, was now governor of Virginia, and with his support the constitutional union was upheld. Madison returned exhausted to his home, which faced the serene distances of the Blue Ridge Mountains.

The thirty miles between Montpellier and Monticello could be driven in one day, and the old tie between Jefferson and Madison was reinforced by the growing affection between Dolley and Jefferson's elder daughter Martha, now the wife of Thomas Mann Randolph, whose father had been a lifelong friend of Jefferson's. There was a bedroom at Monticello which was known as the Madisons', and was kept ready for their occupancy. At Jefferson's request, the young Randolphs and their growing family of children were living at Monticello, even in his absence, but neither Martha Randolph nor her sister Mary, now Mrs. John Eppes, was inclined to accompany him to Philadelphia when he returned to his almost nonexistent duties there.

December of 1799 was saddened by the death of Washington at Mount Vernon, and Jefferson joined the Madisons on a visit of condolence to the widow on the Potomac. Meanwhile Dolley had adjusted with her usual tact and good nature to life under the broad roof of her husband's family, and the senior Madisons had come to love her like another daughter. Madison's "retirement" proved to be pretty much of a myth, as his correspondence with Jefferson was constant and much of his time and thought was devoted to the controversy over the threatening international situation, which Hamilton kept stirring up as the election year of 1800 approached.

This time Jefferson took part in the campaign, in his determination to defeat the reactionary Federalist influence, and he found himself competing for the presidency with Burr, who was anxious to see Hamilton set down. He was deprived of Madison's personal support by the death of the latter's aged father, which obliged Madison to remain at home to settle the estate and keep Montpellier running.

During the summer of 1800 the government moved from Philadelphia to the Potomac site which was to be called Washington in the District of Columbia. Although the public buildings were not finished and few private homes had been built, the winter session of the Sixth Congress under the Constitution convened in the new Capitol Building. Washington, D.C., in 1800 was like a frontier town. The unpaved streets were either deep in dust or mud, and in summer its marshy river-bank location reeked with damp and fog which bred fevers and other ailments in oppressive heat—a climate which has only recently been rendered comfortable by air-conditioned buildings.

The President's House, which was first inhabited by Mr. and Mrs. Adams during the last few months of his presidency, was described by Abigail in a letter to her daughter at that time.

Confiding her housewifely distress at what had been made of a very handsome design—on paper—she wrote:

"In the city there are buildings enough, if they were compact and finished, to accommodate Congress and those attached to it; but as they are, and scattered as they are, I see no great comfort for them. The river, which runs up to Alexandria, is in full view of my window, and I see the vessels as they pass and repass.

"The house is on a grand and superb scale, requiring about thirty servants to attend and keep the separate apartments in order, and perform the ordinary business of the house and stables; an establishment very well proportioned to the President's salary! The lighting of the apartments from the kitchen to parlors and chambers is a tax indeed, and the fires we are obliged to keep to secure us from daily agues is another cheerful comfort! To assist us in this great castle, and render less attendance necessary, bells are wholly wanting, not one single one being hung through the whole house, and promises are all you can obtain. This is so great an inconvenience that I know not what to do, or how to do.

"If they will put me up some bells, and let me have wood enough to keep fires, I design to be pleased. I could content myself almost anywhere for three months; but surrounded with forests, can you believe that wood is not to be had, because people cannot be found to cut and cart it! You must keep all this to yourself, and when asked how I like it say that I write you the situation is beautiful, which is true. The house is made habitable; but there is not a single apartment finished, and all within, except the plastering, has been done since we came. We have not the least fence, yard, or other convenience, without; and the great unfinished audience-room [today the superb white-and-gold East Room] I make a drying-room of, to hang up the wash in. The principal stairs are not up, and will not be this winter. Six chambers are made comfortable. Two are occupied by the President and Mr. Shaw [a secretary]; two lower rooms, one for a common parlor and one for a levee-room. Upstairs there is the oval room, which is designed for the drawing-room, and has the crimson furniture in it. It is a very handsome room now; but when completed it will be beautiful. [This is now the Blue Oval Reception Room.] If the twelve years in which this place has been considered as the future seat of Government had been improved, as they would have been in New England, very many of the present inconveniences would have been removed. It is a beautiful spot, capable of every improvement, and the more I view it, the more I am delighted with it."

The Adamses' sojourn in the President's House was brief and sad. They lost a beloved son Charles that autumn, and another son, John Quincy, was in Europe on a diplomatic post. Abigail, who hated life in the new Federal City, returned to Massachusetts, leaving her husband alone in the bleak, half-furnished mansion with the election roaring all around him.

Both Adams, fighting for reelection, and Jefferson, who had changed his mind in favor of accepting the presidency if he could get it, were well aware that only three electoral votes had separated them four years before, and Burr was running so close to Jefferson in popularity that a tie between them for first place was feared. Burr was charged by his opponents with intriguing against the public will (as well as against Hamilton's, which was not the same thing.) He was then forty-five and at the top of his fortunes. During all the speechmaking and pamphleteering which took the place of radio and television in those days, Burr remained at home with his daughter Theodosia in Albany, where he still held a seat in the New York legislature.

As the electors gathered in the several States, the Federalists prophesied a resounding victory, with Adams reelected for a second term, and Pinckney as vice-president. But the Electoral College vote tied Jefferson and Burr for first place with 73 votes each, Adams 65, and Pinckney 64. This was most embarrassing to the Jeffersonians, and the decision had to be thrown into the House of Representatives, which had a Federalist majority. It was well known that the Federalists preferred anyone, even Burr, to Jefferson.

When the balloting in the House began, thirty-five ballots were taken the first day without any useful change in the total. Nine votes were needed to decide the contest. Jefferson seemed unable to get more than eight, though the obstinate representatives were reminded by the press that "the firm decision of the *people* throughout the United States in favor of Mr. Jefferson" was irresistible.

Caucuses and conferences were held during an adjournment. Hamilton hated Burr even more than he feared Jefferson. When the balloting was resumed, it may have been through his influence that enough votes were shuffled on the thirty-sixth ballot to throw ten to Jefferson, and he was proclaimed president. Burr had lost again, and could claim only the vice-presidency.

Adams did not accord Jefferson the courtesy of attending the inauguration. After packing all night, he drove away towards his Massachusetts home before the city was awake on March 4, 1801.

7

"A Palace in a Forest"

The third President was fifty-eight when he took office, a home-loving widower with two married daughters who would not leave their growing families to keep house for him in the still unfinished President's House in the still unfinished capital city on the Potomac. He was of impressive height, like Washington; slender, sandy-haired, with a husky, untrained speaking voice which put him at a disadvantage in those oratorical times.

Hamilton, whose personal influence with Washington had been exaggerated in order to bring venomous criticism on them both, had lost prestige by the public exposure of a sordid affair with a professional adventuress which had even involved him in blackmail. His wife, who had been Betsy Schuyler before a romantic wartime marriage, stood by him loyally, but his public reputation was hopelessly damaged. Within three years his long, bitter feud with Aaron Burr would end in a tragic duel which caused his death and Burr's everlasting ruin.

Because the opposition party was now in power for the first

time since the government had been formed in 1789, Jefferson had inherited from Adams only Federalist officeholders, and Adams probably felt that the Federalist cause would need all the support he could bequeath to it under a Republican-Democrat president. At that time these two terms, nowadays so opposite, were used almost interchangeably as the opposite to Federalist. "We are all republicans. We are all federalists," Jefferson said in his inauguration speech, appealing for unity against the alternative, which he believed to be anarchy. "If there be any among us who wish to dissolve this union, or to change its republican form, let them stand undisturbed as monuments of the safety with which error of opinion may be tolerated, where reason is left free to combat it."

He would have had to make a clean sweep to assure himself of support on all sides. This he wisely declined to do, believing that "removals must be as few as possible, done gradually, and based on some inherent disqualification." He therefore gathered into his Cabinet only a few special new men he could count on, and among these was James Madison as secretary of state.

The summons was not unexpected at Montpellier, where Madison was still involved in the settlement of his father's estate. He was also in one of his recurrent periods of ill health, and Jefferson paid him a visit in April on the way back to Monticello from Washington after the inauguration. Adams had often left the government to run itself while he went home to Braintree, and Jefferson felt that even a new presidency would survive his occasional sojourn at Monticello. The Madisons followed him on his return to Washington in May, travelling over terrible roads which threatened to overturn their carriage. Madison took the oath of office as secretary of state the day after they arrived.

To understand the unique career of Dolley Madison as it

was now to develop, it is necessary to consider the new nation, the new city, the new century, and the changing times in which she lived. It was natural that she and Madison, accompanied as usual by Anna and little Payne and various servants, should join the solitary president in the bleak executive mansion which stood at the opposite end of Pennsylvania Avenue from the new Capitol Building, which at that time had only one wing completed for use. The white Capitol on its little hill was flanked by the square brick Treasury Building, and the State and War Offices were then combined under one roof.

There were a few private houses clustered on Capitol Hill. New Jersey Avenue, running south towards the Eastern Branch of the Potomac (sometimes called the Anacostia River), had houses on both sides of the road, but ended abruptly above the steep river bank. These buildings were most of them designed as lodgings for the legislators who had not yet begun to build their own homes and bring their families to live in the capital city. Among them stood the mansion built for his wife by Thomas Law, who had married Martha Washington's granddaughter Eliza Custis. The only other built-up section was the single highway (now Washington's M Street) which ran westward through the woods to Georgetown on the other side of Rock Creek, a long established little city which contained some very fine residences.

Between the President's House and the Capitol ran the mile and a half of unpaved roadway called Pennsylvania Avenue, cut through the woods and alder swamps. Beside it there had been laid a stone-paved footway, for the so-called avenue itself was often impassable to carriages in wet weather. There were no houses there, except an occasional workman's shack, and the avenues which according to the grandiose ground-plan of the architects were to radiate from it still showed the stumps of the trees which had been cut down to mark the way.

The amusing diplomat-wit Gouverneur Morris, who had gone to Washington from Philadelphia to witness Jefferson's inauguration, remarked of the new capital: "We only need here houses, cellars, kitchens, scholarly men, amiable women, and a few other such trifles to possess a perfect city. In a word, this is the best city in the world to live in—in the future."

The President's House was built of buff sandstone, which stood out against the brick of the Treasury Building and some private dwellings, and it was called the White House even before it was rebuilt and painted white after the 1814 fire. It stood isolated, as Abigail Adams had said, in a sort of pasture with no fence or protection of any kind. Jefferson at once described it irritably as "a great stone house big enough for two emperors, one Pope, and the Grand Lama into the bargain," and he appointed Benjamin Latrobe to assist him in making it more habitable than the Adamses had left it. It was also described by a British visitor as "a palace in a forest." The original design, by an Irish architect named James Hoban, was more or less copied from the manor houses of England and Ireland, ancestral homes of wealthy 18th-century gentlemen accustomed to ease and dignity and an army of servants.

Apparently no provision had been made by the planners for furnishing the mansion the president was to occupy. The frugal Adamses seem to have got along in a few of the smaller rooms with furniture transported from Philadelphia when the government moved to Washington. Jefferson is known to have had some pieces brought all the way from Monticello to make himself more comfortable in the echoing spaces of his official residence.

Jefferson lacked stables, office space, privacy, and any form of sanitation, as the White House waste was carried by an open wooden sewer which discharged at the surface. For stables and office room Jefferson had designed two one-story colonnaded wings, which Latrobe considered old-fashioned. But within the next few years the sewer was covered over, a stone wall was built to enclose the grounds, and a connecting road to the surrounding avenues was constructed to provide a more suitable approach to the executive mansion. Grading and gardening was begun inside the wall, and a view to the river was opened to the south. Latrobe objected to the basic design of the White House, which was not in accord with his classic ideas. He designed a semicircular portico on the south and a bolder main entrance portico on the north with a porte-cochere—a covered carriage porch. These exterior features appealed to Jefferson, and work on their foundations was begun at once, though they were not completed when his second term ended in 1809. Latrobe was, however, prevented by lack of funds from making alterations to the interior of the house which would have abolished the delightful oval rooms which are still one of its most attractive features.

Jefferson was never a wealthy man, and Monticello claimed most of his available funds, so it did not occur to him to buy what was needed to make the palace a home. This was where Dolley came in, with her genius for hospitality and making people comfortable, and Jefferson was thankful to call on her for assistance in his solitary state. If the vice-president had had a wife, she would have outranked Dolley as the wife of the secretary of state, but Burr was also a widower and in his disappointment took little interest in the duties and privileges of his secondary office. Dolley was therefore free to dispose the scanty furnishings to the best advantage and add what inexpensive domestic touches she could contrive in the bare, formal rooms.

Because the building was gutted by fire in 1814 and all its records and contents perished then, it is difficult to reconstruct either its early interior appearance or the life which was lived within its walls. After their first spartan visit at the beginning of Jefferson's administration, during which time Dolley first took her place as the president's hostess in the absence of his daughters, the Madisons moved into temporary quarters near what is now Washington Circle, where Pennsylvania Avenue became the country road to Georgetown, and Madison set up his office there. His health was still poor, and he longed to escape to the pure air of Montpellier, which he was not able to do until July.

It was considered permissible for the president to absent himself from Washington during the hot summer months, and both Madison and Jefferson conducted the business of government from their respective Virginia homes, connected by a private courier service between Montpellier and Monticello, and a frequent exchange of visits. A note from Jefferson to Madison is typical of the relationship between them at this point. "We shall be happy to see Mrs. Madison and yourself tomorrow," Jefferson wrote, "and shall wait dinner for you till half past four, believing you will easily reach this before that hour. My ford has been a little injured by the freshet, but is perfectly safe. It has a hollow of about nine inches deep and six feet wide, washed in one place exactly in the middle of the river, but even in that it will not be to the belly of the horse. I salute you with great affection and respect."

Diplomats, travellers, and public men, as well as personal friends were glad to escape the city themselves, and flowed through both houses in a constant stream. Among them were the British chargé d'affaires and various members of Congress, who wrote down their impressions in letters which have survived. One of them said of Madison: "He was a man of wit, relished it in others, and his small bright blue eyes would twinkle most wickedly when lighted up by some whimsical conception or association."

Before he left Washington, Madison had instructed the amateur architect Dr. William Thornton to provide a suitable residence for the secretary of state, which could be rented by him. Thornton was in the real estate business, and had built his own house on what is now F Street near 14th Street, besides some other buildings in the Capitol Hill area designed to be let as dwellings to congressmen and diplomats. When the Madisons returned to Washington in October they found their house awaiting them, next door to Thornton's home. The coach house and stabling for four horses were still unfinished, but Thornton had succeeded in removing the secretary of state from the Georgetown trend which was drawing diplomats and executives westward from the President's House. With Madison and his congenial wife located two blocks east of the executive mansion, in the Thornton neighborhood, the social center soon began to take root between there and the Capitol, as Thornton and his various associates had always intended.

The Thorntons proved to be delightful neighbors, and frequent calls for tea-drinking and gossiping were exchanged by the womenfolk. At one time Madison and Thornton jointly owned and raced a horse called Wild Medley, and both were connoisseurs of champagne. Their wives borrowed each other's servants and silver for their entertainments, and the residence of the secretary of state was soon second only to the White House for social popularity.

A member of Congress who dined with the Madisons in F street apparently encountered southern cooking for the first time, and was impressed by the "excellent dinner" provided at Dolley's bountiful table. He preserved the menu in a letter to his wife: "The round of beef of which the soup was made is called 'bouilli.' It had in the dish spices, and something of the sweet herb and garlic kind, and a rich gravy. It is very much boiled and still very good. We had a dish with what appeared to be cabbage, much boiled, then cut in long strings and some-what mashed; in the middle a large ham, with the cabbage around. It looked like our country dishes of bacon and cabbage, with the cabbage mashed up after being boiled till sodden and turned dark. The dessert good; much as usual except two dishes which appeared like apple pie in the form of the half of a musk melon, the flat side down, top creased deep, and the color a dark brown."

In view of what was in store for her after her husband became the fourth president in 1809, these were simple, happy days for Dolley in the F Street house. Even then, her social genius began to shine in the barren, unfinished Washington scene. Abigail Adams had been bored and homesick in the new Federal City, and she always lacked Dolley's outgoing approach to the people she met. Mrs. Margaret Bayard Smith, wife of the man who owned and published the first newspaper in the capital, *The National Intelligencer*, kept up a lively correspondence recording her impressions of the new society into which she had been cordially welcomed when she arrived from Philadelphia. Like everyone else, she became very fond of Dolley Madison, and after dining at the President's House, where Dolley presided as hostess, Mrs. Smith wrote: "I happened to sit next to Mr. Jefferson and was confirmed in my prepossessions in his favor by his easy, candid, and gentle manner. Before and after dinner Mrs. Cranch and myself sat in the drawing-room with Mrs. Madison and her sister, whose social dispositions soon made us well acquainted with each other."

In the warmth of Dolley's presence, Mrs. Smith seems not to have noticed that the mansion was still sparsely furnished, chiefly by things which could be spared from Monticello, along with Jefferson's many books and "collections" of fossils and agricultural specimens. Jefferson's dinner table, like the

Madisons', was bountiful with southern delicacies, prepared by his own servants from Monticello, and presidential formality was considerably relaxed from the court-like etiquette which came naturally to the Washingtons, and the stiff ceremoniousness dictated by John Adams's self-importance. Dinner was customarily served in the middle of the afternoon, and often lasted well into the evening, while the guests conversed easily with each other, drank numerous toasts, and nibbled at nuts and raisins and sweets.

Jefferson let it be known that in addition to his dinner parties and in place of the formal "levees" or receptions held by Washington and Adams, he would receive personally anyone who wished to visit him on two days each year—January 1 and July 4. On these occasions in particular he had need of an experienced hostess with a knowledge of people of all degrees and a memory for names and faces. Here Dolley shone "incomparable." She and Anna had long since abandoned Quaker dress, and their clothes came from Philadelphia before dressmakers' shops were established in Washington which could provide the painted fans, gilded slippers, spangled scarves, plumed bonnets, and elaborate headdresses which fashion required. The Philadelphia dressmakers were able to make up gowns in the European style by copying from carefully dressed dolls which were sent from London and Paris for that purpose.

In the absence of fashion magazines or illustrated periodicals, everyone asked, "What did Mrs. Madison wear?" Once it was a white satin dress, with capes trimmed with swansdown, and a turban of white satin with three large ostrich feathers hanging over her face—"very becoming indeed!" the account concluded. "She looked remarkably well, and as much like a bride as a queen, for she wore no colors." Dolley's costumes for State occasions were often white, though she was never averse to bright colors, especially yellow. She and her sister were soon setting the style for all Washington, and Madison's modest fortune was generously used to provide them with the latest finery. His personal extravagance was a well-stocked wine cellar, though his own abstemiousness was such that some people noticed that he often seemed only to touch the glass to his lips.

Men had now adopted the habit of smoking "segars," and Madison was one of these. Many of them still preferred the eighteenth-century snuff, which was powdered tobacco variously scented and taken in little pinches up the nose from between forefinger and thumb, out of small ornamental boxes carried in their pockets. The dandies made quite a gesture of the performance, flicking open the lid of the box with one hand, and dipping out a few grains with the other in a practiced flourish. It became smart for ladies to indulge in snuff-taking, and the graceful offer and acceptance of snuff from an open box was a common form of ice-breaking in the best society, much as the exchange and lighting of cigarettes became later. Dolley used snuff constantly, till her finger tips were stained with it, and as when women first began to smoke in public, she was sometimes criticized for a habit which a few people considered unbecoming in a female.

For some unaccountable reason, Dolley never learned to dance, although she attended the dancing assemblies in full dress and never lacked for attendants who were happy to sit beside her while others performed the elaborate quadrilles and cotillions which had begun to replace the country dances and the stately minuet, and which were soon to give way to the romping early waltzes. She played the card games of the time—loo and whist—drove round in her carriage with Anna paying calls, leaving cards, and drinking tea—and thoroughly enjoyed the horse races which were something like a picnic attended by all grades of society from top to bottom and white to black, in a sort of annual summer festival. The ladies' carriages were drawn up close to the track, where they could chat to each other and partake of refreshments which they brought with them in hampers, to be dispensed by their own servants. The gentlemen, mounted on their shining thoroughbreds, circulated among the carriages and along the track as patrons of the sport and owners of the race horses.

Gilbert Stuart, whose portraits of the first president were his chief claim to fame, became "all the rage" in the capital city when he set up a studio there, and everyone sat for him, including the Madisons. His portrait of Dolley, painted when she was a ripe thirty-six, is the earliest likeness of her by a well-known artist. It shows her wearing the high-waisted Empire-style gown, her hair in ringlets on her forehead, and the corners of her mouth lifted in the friendly closed smile which all artists, all her life, would take pains to record. The portrait of Madison taken at the same time shows his habitual dark garb, silvered hair, and snowy ruffles at his throat.

During the first autumn of Jefferson's presidency, in 1802, his daughters were kind enough to pay him a visit, and Dolley was called upon to see that they were fashionably dressed and presented to all the right people, and encouraged to enjoy themselves. She loved shopping, and was of almost the same age as Martha Randolph, and she found it a great pleasure to introduce her Virginia friends into Washington society. But the sisters' stay was brief, and they soon returned to their families, leaving the president to manage as best he could with the aid of the most accomplished hostess in Washington, which Dolley had now become.

8

Illness and Separation

As secretary of state, Madison was increasingly involved in the tension which was building up over the western lands, whose rights he and Jefferson had always favored against the northern and Tidewater indifference. During 1802 the territory called Louisiana became a vital and dangerous problem. The mighty Mississippi River flowed along its eastern boundary serving as a trade route for the pioneers and fur traders, who floated their goods down the Ohio River into the Mississippi and so to the port of New Orleans and the Gulf of Mexico. For years the land west of the Mississippi had belonged to Spain, which permitted the use of the river and the port city by the United States settlers in the Ohio region.

Suddenly, it seemed, the French dictator Napoleon Bonaparte had acquired Louisiana from Spain and the port was closed, to the despair of the traders who had no other outlet. It was feared that Bonaparte might intend to establish an aggressive French colonial empire there which would threaten the peaceful expansion of United States citizens westward. Ohio,

Kentucky, and Tennessee were now fully fledged states in the Union, Indiana and Mississippi were territories capable of becoming states, and the Ohio River was their lifeline to New Orleans, by way of the Mississippi. Florida was still under Spanish rule, along with the whole Pacific coast country and Texas. The vast land between the Mississippi and the Rocky Mountains was all called Louisiana, and its actual dimensions and boundaries were unknown to the maps of the period. To have it claimed by a despotic power like Bonaparte's France endangered the freedom and rights of all the American settlements adjoining the Mississippi on the east, and caused instant concern and apprehension in Washington.

The third "Virginia musketeer," James Monroe, had just finished his term as governor when Jefferson appointed him minister plenipotentiary to France to negotiate a purchase from Bonaparte of the Mississippi navigation rights, including the free use of New Orleans, and possibly in addition to acquire a tract of land on which to establish a United States trading post. For these rights the Congress had appropriated two million dollars—though Monroe was secretly authorized to offer up to ten million.

Needless to say, the negotiations were complicated and lengthy, and Madison was in the midst of them as Jefferson's right-hand man. Correspondence was often conducted in cipher, and the Virginia triumvirate was drawn still closer together by Monroe's responsibilities in France, where he was hindered by the jealousy of the resident United States minister, Robert Livingston. Monroe was finally granted an interview with Bonaparte and apparently made a good impression, though nothing was settled between them then. Eventually the American diplomats were astounded to be offered the whole Louisiana Territory, from the mouth of the Mississippi to the Rocky Mountains, where Spanish rule began. Bonaparte had given up his dream of colonial empire in America after a slave rebellion in Santo Domingo, which ended the French hold on the Caribbean. He was shrewd enough to realize that with Santo Domingo gone, Louisiana was "already lost," and moved quickly to make what profit he could from his claim on the mainland. Within a year Bonaparte was to proclaim himself emperor of France, and the new French Republic, so savagely won by the guillotine, came to an end. The United States was then left as the sole representative of true liberty and human rights, and had become a factor to be reckoned with even in the European world.

By exceeding their authorization, the American Commission in France concluded a deal for approximately fifteen million dollars through an English banking firm, and at one stroke doubled the area of the United States. The Federalist party in Congress protested paying such a price for "a worthless wilderness," but in December of 1803 the United States took formal possession of Louisiana, and the following year one of the commissioners at New Orleans, William Claiborne, was installed as the first governor. Florida remained outside the deal, for it was not really Bonaparte's to sell, and Spain was in no mood to let it go.

In April, 1804, a great change took place in Dolley's life, with the marriage of Anna Payne, her "sister-child" and dear companion, to Richard Cutts, a Democratic congressman whose home was in faraway Maine. Cutts was a handsome, cultivated man who had been considered a great beau among the Washington belles, and except that Anna would no longer be a member of the Madison household Dolley had every reason to be happy about the match.

Several letters have survived of the many which passed between the sisters during Anna's wedding journey through

New York and Boston to her husband's home, during the summer of 1804. Dolley always wrote discreetly, even to Anna, with only a passing reference to such events as the shocking Burr-Hamilton duel, which must have been of the keenest interest and perhaps sorrow to those who had known Burr intimately at Philadelphia. The Madisons went to Montpellier as usual that summer, and were deluged with "company," even during a painful illness which prostrated Dolley for days with a form of rheumatic fever.

Just as Anna's new life began, the death of his younger daughter Maria Eppes brought tragedy to Jefferson, who remained with her at Monticello in daily attendance at her bedside, as he had always done during her mother's last illness. It was an election year again, however, and his presence was soon required in Washington, where the great Louisiana Purchase was still being discussed and digested. Federalists were determined to oust him from office and he was equally determined on a second term. Dolley's social grace, tact, and unbiased good humor which steered the presidential entertainments clear of jealousy and controversy were of the greatest value now to the beleaguered president. Her wise and dignified conduct after being suddenly thrust into the limelight was evidence of her strong character and gentle Quaker background. To make up for Anna's absence, she brought from Hanover County a namesake and country cousin, Dolly Winston, who proved to be a faithful and loving companion.

As the election campaigning began again, it was quite plain that Vice-President Burr was no longer a candidate for anything but obscurity, since what many people considered the murder of his old rival Alexander Hamilton on the dueling ground, where Hamilton was supposed to have fired into the air as he received his death wound. Burr had completely disappeared for a discreet interval after the duel, giving it "time to blow over," before he was again seen in Washington. He was then invited to formal affairs at the President's House and the Madisons' in F Street, but it was made quite clear to him that no closer association would be welcome. It was doubtless this polite indifference on the part of many old friends which provided the unfortunate man with what he considered grounds for his withdrawal into intrigues which later brought him to trial for treason.

Jefferson was re-elected, with the aging George Clinton of New York as vice-president and the Republican party in full control of Congress. Clinton was too old to aspire to the presidency after another four years, and the succession was now plain to everyone. Burr was done for as a contestant, and Jefferson clearly intended that Madison should follow him as the fourth president. The prospect was not an altogether happy one for Dolley, who had no social ambition and knew only too well the grinding responsibilities of the office, and had already experienced the doubtful advantages of acting as hostess for the president. Madison's health was always chancy, and his public service had already demanded too much of him. He longed for the peace and quiet of Montpellier, and the life of a gentleman farmer, as he chose to think of himself. But he was younger than Jefferson, and more popular than Monroe, and—he had Dolley. The writing was already on the wall when Jefferson was inaugurated for the second time in 1805.

A mysterious illness overpowered Dolley that summer, described vaguely as "a sore on her knee"—some sort of infection which kept her in bed while various "fierce" remedies were tried. She went to the July 4 reception at the White House, "sitting still, and amusing myself with the mob," she wrote Anna. She had a visit from her sister Lucy's husband George Steptoe Washington and his brother Lawrence, which enlivened the household with "Virginia hilarity," though

George was already showing signs of the "consumption" which would cause his early death.

When the infection in Dolley's knee did not improve—and in those days there was always the dread of gangrene setting in—Madison insisted on consulting a Quaker doctor in Philadelphia, a colleague of the famous Dr. Rush, who had the appropriate name of Philip Syng Physick, and was destined to be known as the Father of American Surgery.

They set out for Philadelphia instead of making their usual summer journey to Montpellier. Madison would not leave his wife, although her old friends all rallied to her bedside in the "excellent lodgings" they found in Sansom Street. Dolley wrote to Anna that she had been "lectured" by an old Quaker acquaintance "for seeing too much company, and it brought to my mind the time when our Society used to control me entirely and debar me from so many advantages and pleasures; and although so entirely removed from their clutches, I really felt my ancient terror of them revive to a disagreeable degree. Madison is well, though besieged with callers; he sends his love to you both, as I do." Facing the future years of increasing responsibility, Dolley could at least look back and regard her busy life as an escape from the restrictions amounting to tyranny which had ruled her youth.

Montpellier had to run itself that summer, for the treatment which restored Dolley to health and activity lasted three months, some of the time with her leg in splints. In October Madison was called back to Washington to confer with Jefferson on the alarming developments abroad, which threatened the neutrality of the United States in the perpetual war between France and England. It was the first and almost the only separation of the Madisons' married life, and Dolley was writing to him almost before he was out of sight. "A few hours only have passed since you left me, my beloved, and I find nothing can relieve the oppression of my mind but speaking to you in this, the only way. I shall feel better when Peter [the coachman] returns with news, not that any length of time will lessen my first regret, but an assurance that you are well and easy will contribute to make me so." She added a postscript the next day: "The watchman announced a cloudy morning at one o'clock, and from that moment I found myself unable to sleep, from anxiety for thee, my dearest husband. Detention, cold, and accident seem to menace thee." And the next day: "This cold, clear morning will favor your journey and enliven the feelings of my darling. The knee is mending, and I sit just as you left me. The doctor, during his short visits, talks of you. Adieu, my beloved, our hearts understand each other."

Dolley's few surviving letters to her husband are evidence of the deep love she felt for the small, unimpressive man with the twinkling blue eyes who seemed to possess so little of the showy masculine magnetism which was characteristic of many men of the period. She worried incessantly about his health, while her own was a source of real anxiety to him. She followed in her mind's eye every mile of the journey which took him from her, and regretted that the last part of it must be made by the public stage, while the coachman brought the carriage back to Philadelphia. In her bad dreams she saw him ill and helpless at home, without her there to tend him, though he was served by a devoted colored body servant. They were love letters, full of endearments not usually committed to paper in those more formal times, even between husband and wife. She had been married to him more than ten years, and they had no children of their own, although he always treated her wilful little son Payne as his.

Dolley was thirty-seven, he was fifty-four. And in the midst of his preoccupations as secretary of state in anxious days, his own letters to her were equally ardent: "Yours of the 1st inst., my dearest, gives me much happiness, but it cannot be complete till I have you with me. ...." And Dolley replied: "I have at this moment perused with delight thy letter, my darling husband, with its enclosures. To find that you love me, have my child safe, and that my mother is well, seems to comprise all my happiness. I am getting well as fast as I can, for I have the reward in view of seeing my beloved. Tell me if Mrs. Randolph is expected, and all the news you have time and patience to give me. I have written you every day since we parted, but am so shut up that I can say nothing to amuse; when I begin to drive out, I hope to become a more interesting correspondent." A few days later: "I walk about the room, and hope a few days more will enable me to ride, so that you may expect me to fly to you as soon—ah! I wish I might say how soon! It is now past nine o'clock, and I cease to write, only to dream of thee. Tell Mrs. Thornton I am having the model of a bonnet made for her; the new ones are just coming in. Write soon to thy devoted DOLLEY."

Mrs. Martha Randolph was coming to Washington to spend the winter with her father—her second visit there—and Dolley in Philadelphia where the dressmakers were was requested by the president to oversee the outfitting of the country visitors with the latest fashion in gowns, bonnets, scarves, slippers, etc. Jefferson was often criticized for the carelessness of his own dress, and had even worn his riding clothes into formal company. His daughter Martha was always lacking in style, but he admired Dolley's natural elegance and Madison's habitual neat attire, and he doubtless thought the invitation to costume Mrs. Randolph and her attendant daughters would prove a welcome stimulant to Dolley's convalescence. Dolley was delighted, for she loved to shop, and had herself driven round to all the best establishments where selected articles were brought out to the carriage for her approval, as she was unable to leave it and walk about. She carried the new bonnet she had had made for Mrs. Thornton in a bandbox all the way to Washington in the carriage driven by her husband's coachman, behind a handsome pair of new horses provided to celebrate her recovery.

Anna and her husband joined her in Philadelphia and rode with her when she returned in triumph to the F Street house and her many duties there. Even her fear of a lingering lameness had been dispelled by Dr. Physick's treatment.

It was an unusually brilliant social season in the capital. Mrs. Randolph presided for the first and only time as hostess at her father's New Year's Day reception. She had brought her son and five daughters with her, so that an echo of Monticello family life was heard in the lonely executive mansion. But Dolley Madison was still needed there, from the nursery to the dinner table, especially as Mrs. Randolph's visit was interrupted, or complicated, by the birth of another son, who was named James Madison Randolph. He was the first child to be born in the first White House.

Anna Cutts as a married woman shared with Dolley the chaperonage of the Randolph daughters, who were now making their début. There is a legend that their dear, dowdy, nearsighted mother attended a ball where she failed to recognize her own daughter Anne, who had been transformed into beauty overnight by Dolley's skill and example.

It was at this time that Aaron Burr made one of his rare reappearances in Washington, with his daughter Theodosia, now Mrs. Joseph Alston of South Carolina. They were received everywhere with courtesy if not cordiality. Burr was even then maturing his fantastic dream of a western empire beyond the Alleghenies, divorced from the Washington administration and ruled entirely by himself—a mad conspiracy of dupes and diehard Federalists which when it became known would ruin him. Apparently Jefferson did know what he was up to, and wisely allowed him enough rope before ordering his arrest at Natchez in 1807. On this subject, and the sensational trial at Richmond where Burr won a grudging acquittal from treason, Dolley maintained her usual discreet silence. It is possible that in her secret thoughts she wondered at the legendary Inner Light which had guided her choice between this irresponsible charmer and the sober, kindly man she had married.

9

President
James Madison

As Jefferson's second term drew to a close, the neutrality which he, like Washington, considered essential to the survival of the new nation became more perilous than ever before, pinched between the two warring powers of France and England. There was also the perpetual dispute over Florida, which was claimed by Spain, but which was now surrounded by United States territory. Monroe was sent on to Madrid to try to repeat his Louisiana success, but Bonaparte was not pleased at what he considered American presumption, and refused to exert his influence in Monroe's favor. The King of Spain claimed to be "Emperor of the American Indies," including most of the islands and Florida. Alarmed by the Louisiana Purchase, he reinforced his garrisons in Texas, and tensions on the Gulf and the west bank of the Mississippi were created, while Spanish privateers began to operate in the Caribbean. Once again a dangerous balance existed—the United States threatened by a possible alliance between France and Spain, which feared its growing power—or a possible United States alliance with England, which might seize that opportunity to embarrass its European enemies.

Monroe left Spain with nothing accomplished and went to England, for Jefferson wanted an ally somewhere in Europe—almost any ally—and hoped that England might back him up in Florida because of its eternal quarrel with France. But England had now become desperate for manpower, and adopted a piratical practice of searching American ships at sea for supposed English deserters from the war. During the process of search they often seized men who were actually American citizens and impressed them into the English services, and even brought American ships into British harbors as prizes in a form of piracy which raised Madison's indignation and caused a good deal of angry and fruitless negotiation and diplomatic controversy. Nelson had made England mistress of the seas. Bonaparte was in control of the Continent. Between the two, defending its rights as a free nation, stood the United States of America.

In spite of a lot of hotheaded talk in Congress about seizing Florida by force, Jefferson switched round to conciliation, and offered to purchase the territory for two million dollars. For the first time a split developed in the Republican party, led by the neurotic John Randolph of Roanoke, Virginia, who violently attacked the policies of Jefferson and Madison, and backed Monroe, who he said had been helpless to achieve anything within the limits of their instructions to him. This put a strain on the friendship between Madison and Monroe, who acted with loyalty and dignity in the embarrassing situation thrust upon him.

Then, in the summer of 1807 an incident on the high seas created a new crisis. The British cruiser *Leopard* attempted to board and search the American frigate *Chesapeake* in the waters off Cape Henry, Virginia. The captain of the *Chesa-*

*peak*e resisted, and his ship was fired on and crippled. The British then boarded her and removed four men said to be British deserters, who were actually American seamen. The *Chesapeake* struggled back to Norfolk, and a storm of anti-British feeling flared up in America. Jefferson issued a proclamation ordering British warships out of territorial waters, and the British replied with an order for more severe harassment of "neutral" vessels. Jefferson then slapped an embargo on American shipping, which stopped nearly all United States trade with foreign ports and caused immediate financial loss to American merchants and shipowners. A brisk smuggling trade began, and American cargoes caught in foreign ports by the Embargo Act of January, 1808, were confiscated. American industry and commerce suffered severely, and this roused protest in state legislatures, some of which refused to honor the embargo.

Jefferson's desperate attempt to substitute non-intercourse for war was a failure, defeated by public opinion which rose against him with the loss of trade and the spoilage of tobacco, cotton, and rice shipments which rotted on the wharves. A strong anti-embargo, anti-Madison party was created even in the South, where it was headed by John Randolph, threatening Jefferson's hope that his secretary of state would be the next president, and raising up the detached envoy Monroe as a rival candidate for the 1808 election.

Dolley's sister Anna returned to Maine with her husband that summer of 1807, and the Madisons were at Montpellier. Monroe had returned again, heartsick, to his Virginia home, withdrawing from the faction which would have set him up as Madison's rival. Jefferson let him go without a friendly word, preoccupied with his own loss of popularity and the estrangement of friends who felt the economic disaster of the embargo. Like Washington he had refused a third term, and the question of his successor was now complicated by the blame reflected on Madison as his secretary of state in a policy which seemed to have failed. Both Monroe and Clinton were considered more suitable candidates by the anti-Jefferson faction within the Republican party, led by the bitter-tongued John Randolph, who openly preferred Monroe. Clinton was feeble at sixty-eight, but was backed by the New York political machine, which objected to another president from Virginia, in what was beginning to be called "the Virginia Dynasty."

Madison did no campaigning. Monroe refused to oppose him, for the sake of the friendship between them and the already perilous unity of the Republican party. He had taken a house in Richmond and was quietly practicing law there. In spite of frenzied maneuvering by John Randolph, the congressional caucus in January, 1808, nominated Madison with 83 votes out of a possible 94. Clinton was renominated for the vice-presidency, which was now on a separate ballot. Monroe was nowhere, with 3 votes. On the motion of a senator from Virginia Madison's nomination was declared unanimous.

By the time the Madisons reached Montpellier in the summer of 1808, family sorrow still eclipsed every other emotion. Mrs. Payne had died in October at the Clarksburg home of her daughter Mary, who had married Senator John Jackson, and Mary died soon after, having outlived all her children but the youngest. They made the homeward journey in terrible weather, against floods and high winds, and Dolley went down again with inflammatory rheumatism, and was in great pain. They put her to bed, in Dolly Winston's devoted care, and shielded her from the hordes of visitors which descended on the house.

Jefferson stopped there, on his way back to Washington with his secretary. As soon as Dolley was well enough the

Madisons followed him and she cheerfully resumed her duties in the F Steeet house. Because he had worked in Jefferson's shadow and presumably under Jefferson's orders, Madison was bound to inherit Jefferson's enemies, and little was known by the public of his own toil and tact and diplomatic skill in the international embargo tangle. Federalist journalism made the most of what private correspondence and inside rumor it could dredge up to discredit the Jefferson administration. Monroe's conduct abroad was criticized, and the English, French, and Spanish diplomats commented freely, each from his separate bias, on what was after all none of their business—the choice of a new American president.

The electors were chosen in November and returns began coming in from the various states, carried by post or by couriers on horseback. Madison's victory was soon plainly forecast. When the votes were counted in Congress in February, 1809, Madison had a majority of 122 to the Federalist C. C. Pinckney's 47—a vindication of Jefferson's principles and his effort to preserve America's safety in a world at war, with appreciation of Madison's integrity and devotion to his country's welfare. Clinton retained the vice-presidency.

Jefferson was quoted as saying that the country had three choices—embargo, war, or submission to piracy against its ships at sea. No one contemplated the third. The embargo was universally detested. That left Madison facing war. And with both France and England waging what already amounted to war against United States commerce, it looked like war on both hands with the two most powerful nations in Europe.

Congress was "in confusion and perplexity." New England, which had suffered most from the embargo, was talking openly of secession, or preferably war. Jefferson's personal authority, so long maintained, had now vanished, "I verily believe," cried the Pennsylvania lawyer Alexander Dallas, "that one more year of writing and speaking and appointing would render Mr. Jefferson a more odious president, even to the Democrats, than John Adams." And so he was free to return at last to Monticello and his daughter Martha's loving care and the affection of his grandchildren. He was much happier than his friend and colleague through thirty years of political tussle, President-elect James Madison.

The nation itself was full of cheerful satisfaction, the Jeffersonians because he was being followed by his intimate friend, while the Federalists could rejoice because the prime Democrat-Republican was out of office, and the hated embargo was to be lifted so that trade might resume.

10

First Lady

There was a colorful inaugural procession in March, 1809, along Pennsylvania Avenue between Jefferson's newly planted Lombardy poplar trees, to the House of Representatives, which had recently been completed. Salutes of cannon from Fort Washington on the Potomac and the Navy Yard in Washington began at dawn. Troops of uniformed militia appeared to escort the presidential carriage, and thousands of people gathered along the route of the procession to throw up hats and wave handkerchiefs.

Jefferson returned to Washington to witness the ceremony, which took place in what is now known as the Statuary Hall of the Capitol, which was then fitted with drapes and desks as the debating chamber. Madison was observed to be trembling when he began to speak, but steadied as he went on as he always did in any crisis. Dolley was beside him, showing her usual composure and wearing a headdress of nodding plumes which made her appear taller than he was.

The reception was held at their F Street house, which was

thrown open to all who wanted to enter, friends and strangers alike. It was a "great crush," with the street full of carriages and people waiting as much as an hour to enter the crowded rooms. The Madisons stood together at the drawing room door to receive their guests, and Mrs. Smith recorded that Dolley looked "extremely beautiful," and was "dressed in a plain cotton cambric dress with a very long train, plain around the neck without any kerchief, and a beautiful bonnet of purple velvet and white satin, with white plumes. She was all dignity, grace, and affability." Madison had varied his customary black attire by wearing a suit of dark brown merino wool, woven in this country. The Federalist gentlemen wore the bright colors and rich fabrics of the 18th century, while the Republicans followed Jefferson's example of plain American cloth and a minimum of lace at throat and wrists. But the gathering was notable for its fine dresses highlighted by the uniforms and decorations of the army, navy, and the foreign diplomatic corps.

It was Dolley's idea that there should be a gala inauguration ball, a custom which has prevailed ever since. In 1809 it took place at Mr. Long's Hotel on Capitol Hill, which provided a large room with a dance floor, and two fireplaces, so that the atmosphere soon became stifling, till someone purposely broke the upper panes of some sash windows which refused to open and let in some fresh air. The Madisons drove to the ball from the F Street house in a new state carriage drawn by four horses with a coachman in livery on the box. The streets were not paved or lighted, except for the footmen's hand torches, but the windows of the hotel blazed with candlelight from within, and the sound of violins reached the respectful crowd which had gathered outside to see the great folks enter.

Again, Mrs. Smith recorded that Dolley "looked a queen," in a "pale buff-colored velvet gown, made plain, with a very long train, but not the least trimming, and beautiful pearl necklace, earrings, and bracelets. Her headdress was a turban (made in Paris) of the same colored velvet and white satin, with two superb plumes, the bird of paradise feathers. It would be *absolutely impossible* for anyone to behave with more perfect propriety than she did. Unassuming dignity, sweetness, and grace. It seems to me that such manners would disarm envy itself, and conciliate even enemies."

Dolley's pearls were a celebration present from her husband. At supper, Madison escorted sister Anna Cutts, and was seated opposite his wife, who had placed herself between the French and British ministers, and somehow maintained harmony between the two representatives of nations long at war with each other.

To take her already familiar place as the nation's official hostess, a position she had held with grace while Jefferson was president, Dolley simply transplanted her well-organized F Street household into the White House and expanded its usual routine to suit its new station. The man who had acted as her butler in F Street became famous as the White House porter, head steward, or major-domo—"French John" Sioussat. This extraordinary man had found his way to Washington from humble beginnings in Paris, after Bonaparte's elevation to power following the French Revolution. He aspired to become an American, but accepted a position as servant to the French-speaking wife of the British Minister Anthony Merry. He was quick to learn the art of running a fashionable household and soon spoke English adequately. When Mrs. Merry left Washington Dolley somehow acquired Sioussat as a loyal and faithful factotum, and her confidence in him as well as the kindness with which she treated all her employees inspired a loyalty and friendship between them which lasted for years. Another standby whose presence helped to smooth her way was Madison's bachelor secretary Edward Coles, a distant cousin of Dolley's on her mother's side. Coles was soon acting as older brother to her spoilt, wayward son Payne Todd, and he sat at the foot of her table to keep the conversational ball rolling at the large dinner parties which seemed sometimes to eclipse the retiring, soft-spoken president.

The Thorntons were left behind in F Street when the Madisons moved into the house on Pennsylvania Avenue, but the friendship between them was undiminished. The following June Mrs. Thornton recorded in her diary that with the temperature at 90 degrees she had got ice "from the President's." Dolley was still neighborly.

After Abigail Adams's thrifty ways and frugal entertaining, and Jefferson's careless bachelor style, Dolley's regular Wednesday receptions and lavish refreshments were soon famous, both in Washington society and among the diplomatic and foreign visitors, who always made a point of attending and never failed to emerge full of admiration for the handsome, kindly woman who received everyone with her ready, turned-up smile and well-chosen words of welcome. Tirelessly she would move about the rooms which blazed with candlelight, offering her hand or her open snuff-box to old friends and strangers alike, always richly dressed and brilliantly jewelled, skilfully relieving her sometimes exhausted husband of the necessity to lead or animate the conversation. One observer left the comment that: "We remarked on the ease with which she glided into the stream of conversation and accommodated herself to its endless variety. In the art of conversation she is said to be quite distinguished."

The official residence of an elegant, tasteful woman as the president's wife needed to be adorned as a suitable frame for her hospitality, and Congress released the sum of $14,000 from the Treasury to furnish the interior of the White House for the Madisons. Jefferson had been pleased with what Benjamin Latrobe accomplished on his behalf with very little means a few years before, and Dolley had doubtless had a hand in that too. Probably at her request, Latrobe was assigned to the same task again, with money to spend.

He consulted frequently with Dolley, whose ideas usually agreed with his own, and he went shopping for her in Philadelphia and Baltimore for the imported damasks, satins, and velvets which were made up into draperies and upholstery. As his wife was a Philadelphian and an old friend of Dolley's, it is probable that her woman's touch was added to his professional interior decorating. Dolley's desire was simply to make the White House rooms as beautiful and distinguished as possible, not because it was for a time to be her home but because she appreciated the significance and dignity of the presidential office. Carpets, furniture, mantels, lighting fixtures, mirrors, silver plate and china, even table and bed linens were purchased for the mansion from the big shops in Philadelphia, and when he could not find what he wanted Latrobe drew a design and had it made, so that the house acquired a planned and distinguished unity it had never had before. All these beautiful furnishings were to perish in the 1814 fire, though some of Latrobe's drawings for chairs and tables in the classic style popular in Bonaparte's France have survived.

The brocade hangings and upholstery of the drawing room, now the Oval Room, repeated the colors of the carpet which were red, light blue, and yellow, and $450 was expended for an impressive pianoforte as a final touch. The one-time Quakeress was free to enjoy the music and rich colors which had been denied her in her youth. The great full-length Stuart portrait of Washington, after some discussion, was hung in the dining room, where Dolley's receptions were held, and it presided there until in 1814 she herself had it removed beyond the reach of the British army which was marching on the city. Retouched—and spoilt—by a later artist, it hangs now in the white and gold East Room of the White House, which is used for State occasions and formal entertainments.

Dolley looked younger than her thirty-seven years, and dressed handsomely in cheerful colors against her husband's habitual neat black. But it was said that in the privacy of her housewifely mornings she reverted to the plain gray or drab stuff dresses of the Quaker woman, emerging at midday in the butterfly garb which she considered her position as the president's wife required—another evidence of her thoughtful, level-headed acceptance of the obligations, if not the privileges, of the First Lady.

The frequent references by contemporary writers to the lack of "trimming" or kerchief on her formal attire were due to the fact that she and Anna followed the European style of low-cut, high-waisted gowns with short puffed sleeves which left the arms and bosom bare. The change in women's fashions after the French Revolution had been one of the most sudden and drastic in history. In France it had been dangerous to dress in the old court style with powder and hoops and rich brocades. England was quick to follow the new trend. Almost overnight, it seemed, the panniers and stiff satins and filmy fichus above tight bodices gave way to the flimsy, clinging straight gowns made popular on the Continent by the Empress Josephine. Very little was worn under the thin gauze, batiste, cambric, or silk sheaths, and the transparent spangled scarves were draped from the elbows instead of filling in the neckline. There was even for a time a fad in France for damping the fine fabrics to make them still limper so as to cling more closely to the lines of the body, which of course led to colds and respiratory complaints. Women's hair was often cropped short "à la guillotine" and curled in ringlets bound by a wreath of silver leaves or covered by elaborate turban creations. Powder and wigs were no longer worn by the younger men once George IV's Regency began. Madison, like Washington, had always worn his own hair, white from middle age as though powdered, in a short queue tied with a black ribbon. He wore his formal knee-breeches and silk stockings long after gentlemen of fashion had adopted the tight pantaloons which were the forerunners of trousers. His fine lace jabots and wrist ruffles were in elderly contrast to the dandies' starched white neckcloths arranged in a variety of intricate folds and knots which Beau Brummell in England had made an art in itself.

In their private hours together the Madisons were "Dolley" and "Jemmy" to each other, in a period when it was not unusual for a wife to address her husband as "Mr.", and she guarded him in every possible way from his lifelong tendency to overwork, which had wrecked his health during his Princeton College days. He always slept very little, and kept a candle burning all night in his bedchamber, so that he could read or write in his wakeful hours. He said himself that a few minutes in his wife's company, where he was always sure of a new story and some lighthearted laughter, was the greatest refreshment he could find in the midst of his many anxieties. He may never have suspected that it was most of all for his entertainment and relaxation that she surrounded herself with parties of admiring young people and pleasant friends who always felt free to call on her, even after she left the F Street house for the presidential mansion. During the Cabinet meetings, which often went on for hours, Dolley made a habit of inviting the wives of the members to all-female gatherings in her sitting room, called "dove parties," where needlework, knitting, and friendly gossip went on amid the teacups and cake trays.

So for the first time since that bleak dwelling had been erected for the president's accommodation it became a real home, full of warm family feeling, young laughter, and happy faces. Madison was nevertheless often abstracted in society, unless at the end of an informal meal with friends he mellowed and told his rather broad, old-school stories, to the surprise of the younger generation who might be present.

In the midst of all her domestic and official duties Dolley found time to read and used books as a conversational springboard; in particular, *Don Quixote* and the novels of Fenimore Cooper, which latter she complained were "too full of horrors," and other fiction of her day which has now been long forgotten. Her devoted servants were well treated and yet were kept up to the mark.

Clinton of New York had kept the vice-presidency on the Republican ticket, which to our later confusion was still called in those days the Democratic. But the party once so united behind Jefferson's first election against the Federalists had now split up into angry factions, and Madison had not Jefferson's tremendous personal magnetism and influence. It is almost safe to say that the warmhearted, friendly, and hospitable Dolley was more welcome in Washington society as the president's wife than Madison was as the president. She was not a learned or a travelled woman, compared to her "bluestocking" contemporaries, but she was quick to acquire graces and general knowledge from her more sophisticated associates. She had a genuine, outgoing love for all kinds of people, she remembered names and faces, and her spontaneous tact and good will smoothed over many little feuds and differences when they confronted each other in her drawing room to be forgotten, at least temporarily, in the glow of her expansive nature.

The Madisons returned to Montpellier in the summer of 1809 to oversee the completion of the two wings originally designed for the house by Thornton. The elder Mrs. Madison, at seventy-seven, still resided in her separate apartments there, undisturbed by the endless flow of visitors, a few of whom were presented to her as a special privilege.

Mrs. Smith was one of these, and recorded the homelike comfort and lack of ceremony of the Montpellier hospitality. A late breakfast was served to between fifteen and twenty persons, during her stay, and consisted of hot wheat bread, light cakes, a pone or corn loaf, cold ham, chickens, "nice hashes, etc."—with both tea and coffee. Among the guests were the president's brother William and his wife, and Dolley's sister Anna Cutts and her family.

Madison was called back to Washington by the worsening situation with both England and France over commerce on the high seas. The arrival of a new British minister, and the irascible temperament of the resident French minister, promised further complications in the international tangle. These were still unsettled when he and Dolley returned to Montpellier again in the summer of 1810, and there was a continuous war of pamphlets, letters to the newspapers, and intrigue by semi-official correspondence during all that year.

Meanwhile, the Spanish Florida question was hotting up again, particularly in the western part of that territory, which included Mobile and Pensacola. The conviction was growing that "nature has decreed the union of Florida with the United States, and the welfare of the inhabitants demands it." Since Bonaparte had put his brother Joseph on the puppet throne of Spain, the possibility existed that he intended to make Spanish Florida another Louisiana, and this roused the perpetual American dread of either France or England as an aggressive near neighbor on the southern half of the North American continent. As far back as 1808, Jefferson had expressed a desire to exclude all European influence from this hemisphere. In January, 1811, Madison issued a proclamation which foreshadowed what in 1824 would become known as the Monroe Doctrine—

in which he stated that "the United States could not see without serious inquietude any part of a neighboring territory . . . pass from the hands of Spain into those of any other foreign power." Florida was to remain a sore point till 1819.

With Jefferson in retirement at Monticello, James Monroe re-entered the political scene by becoming governor of Virginia for the second time early in 1811. In May of that year he was persuaded by Madison to replace the inept Robert Smith as secretary of state. Jefferson approved the appointment, but Monroe went to Washington with some misgivings, aware that he did not altogether agree with the president's apparent policy of maintaining a precarious peace with France at the expense of strained relations with France's enemy, England, where the Prince Regent had recently taken over the government from the aged, insane George III.

It was soon plain that the Regent intended to retain his father's Ministry, so that the impasse between England and the United States remained unchanged. The American minister in London resigned and came home, as his colleague in France had already done, though the astute French minister, Louis Sérurier, was still busy in Washington on France's behalf. The slow communications of the period prolonged the suspense, and led the uninformed to suppose that Madison was weak and undecided, and that his policies were influenced by his associates. But Sérurier knew Madison by hard experience, and reported briefly to Paris: "Mr. Madison governs by himself."

During the summer of 1811 the additional wings to Montpellier were finished, and both Monroe and Jefferson were guests there. Their visits were returned as usual by the Madisons.

"We passed two months on our mountain in health and peace," Dolley wrote to the wife of the poet-politician Joel Barlow, who had been sent as minister to France, "returning the first of October to a sick and afflicted city. The unfinished canal caused a bilious fever to prevail through all its streets; many died, and Congress convened in dread of contagion. Happily all fear is over now, and business engrosses them very thoroughly. We have new members in abundance, with their wives and daughters, and I have never felt the entertainment of company oppressive until now.

"As you, my dear friends, have everything and we nothing that is beautiful, I will ask the favor of you to send me by a safe vessel some large headdresses, a few flowers, feathers, gloves, and stockings, black or white, with anything else pretty, and suitable for an economist, and let me know the amount. We have a house full of company, and I must conclude with love and prayers for you all, my best friends— Affectionately ...."

A letter to her from Mrs. Barlow mentions her intention to send "some pretty things which are in high style here, gold and silver embroidery done with silk on mull." Mull was a thin, soft muslin made in India, very suitable for the clinging gowns of the period.

The first cold weather had ended the epidemic of "bilious fever," but the inhabitants of Washington remained uneasy, suspicious, and divided in their political opinions.

On the western frontier the Shawnee chief Tecumseh was organizing the Indian tribes to resist the white settlers' advance into what the Indians considered their own land, and it was suspected that he was encouraged by the British governor in Canada. General William Henry Harrison, governor of the Indiana Territory, led a small army against Tecumseh and defeated him in the battle of Tippecanoe on the Wabash River, in November, 1811.

The twelfth Congress, which met in the autumn of the same year, had a choice between war with England and war with

France, with some reckless advocates for a triangular war with both. The United States was still caught in the middle, desperate for trade and unable to protect its ships at sea from piracy on both sides. "The present situation of the world is indeed without parallel, and that of our own country is full of difficulties," Madison had said in his inaugural address. Today, a hundred and fifty-eight years later, things look just about the same.

The general belief that the British in Canada were involved in a conspiracy with the Indians against United States westward expansion increased the hostility between the two nations. But Madison would hardly have been brought to declare war if it had not been for Britain's persistent interference with American commerce at sea. The British Navy continued to blockade American ports, seize American ships, confiscate their cargoes, and carry off men from their crews to serve under the British flag, on the pretense that they were deserters from the British forces.

Dolley watched the approach of war with the deepest anxiety, aware of the exhausting efforts of her husband to avert a conflict. During the tense winter of 1811-12 she brought into the household her widowed sister Lucy Washington from Harewood and young Phoebe Morris, daughter of the Quaker Anthony Morris who had witnessed her wedding to John Todd in Philadelphia. Phoebe had been raised in a small town in Pennsylvania where her mother had died. She was quaint and charming in her simple Quaker ways, and was dazzled by her first glimpse of the great world of society where Dolley reigned. The more sophisticated Lucy was an attractive widow of thirty-five, who soon became a popular belle with many suitors. From among these, with unexpected good sense, she chose a justice of the Supreme Court, a widower with several children, an unrelated Todd.

In March of 1812 Dolley wrote to their sister Anna Cutts, whose husband was confined to their home in Maine with an injury to his shoulder:

"Before this reaches you, my beloved sister Lucy will be married to Judge Todd of Kentucky. Their home is to be in Lexington, but as a Supreme Judge he is obliged to come here for two months every winter, and binds himself to bring her to her friends when she pleases to come. You may imagine my grief is not slight at the parting, and Lucy too is in deep distress. . . .

"But how wise she is to choose him, in preference to the gay ones who courted her. Mr. Madison thinks that ere long the Supreme Judges may be obliged to live at or near the seat of Government. I will write to you, dear Anna, every day that I can take up my pen, and am prepared with a room and every attention for your husband; he will be here, I hope, in time to give his vote for war. However, I may be mistaken, and that dreaded epoch may be some distance off."

Lucy's was the first wedding to take place in the White House, but it was a quiet one and soon forgotten.

The least warlike of men, scholarly, frail in health, of a gentle, reflective nature, Madison might have succeeded somehow in threading his diplomatic way through the recurrent crises if only England had left off its obstinate, bungling, inexcusable interference with American ships and seamen. But in April, 1812, his message to Congress requested an immediate embargo for sixty days, which was extended to ninety days by Congress at the same time it gave him the power to call up 100,000 militia for a limited period of time. The assassination of the British Prime Minister Spencer Perceval in London opened the way for concessions or a change of policy by the British government, but the news of Perceval's death did not reach Washington in time. On the fourth of June, 1812, the

House declared war on England by a vote of 79 to 49. On the seventeenth the Senate voted for war, 19 to 13.

Once again, after years of peace and growing prosperity, the New World faced the Old, on its own ground as before, and with untrained troops and a very limited navy. Since England was already entangled in a war with Bonaparte on the Continent, it was obvious that she could not commit her full force to a new conflict across the Atlantic. But popular opinion in America was violently divided, and in New England where merchant shipowners only wanted to appease England and save their trade abroad, the embargo was as unpopular as it had been in Jefferson's time. Federalists spoke bitterly of "Mr. Madison's war," and accused the president of partiality towards the French, whose behavior at sea was almost as provocative as England's.

The nearest British were in Canada, and the Tippecanoe affair still rankled, so preparations were made at Washington to invade Canada from Lake Champlain and Detroit. The Indians of course joined with the British, and the Canadian campaign soon became a disaster for the United States. Commodore Oliver Perry's decisive victory over a British fleet on Lake Erie in September, 1813, was the only consolation.

By his declaration of war in June Madison risked the loss of a second term, as 1812 was an election year. A campaign of violent abuse was launched against him, in which the sober, abstemious man was accused of drunkenness after dinner, and the use of opium "for pains in his teeth." In the confused and divided state of the Congress and the country these wild fabrications were actually believed and handed on in the frantic attempt to discredit him. Jefferson from his retirement at Monticello replied to one of these slanders which had been repeated to him in a letter from a friend: "You probably may not know Mr. Madison personally, or at least as intimately as I do. I have known him since 1779, when he first came into the public councils; and from three and thirty years' trials, I can conscientiously say that I do not know a man in the world of purer integrity, more disinterested and devoted to genuine republicanism than himself; nor could I, in the whole scope of America and Europe, point out an abler head. He may be illy seconded by others, but what man can do will be done by Mr. Madison. I hope, therefore, that there will be no differences among Republicans as to his re-election, for we shall only appreciate his true value when we have to give him up and look at large for a successor."

When November came and the ballots were cast, Madison won an easy victory over DeWitt Clinton of New York, nephew to the vice-president, who had lately died in office. Elbridge Gerry of Massachusetts became vice-president. Monroe remained as secretary of state. The country may not have liked the idea of war, but it believed in Madison.

Meanwhile Dolley's famous Wednesday receptions continued to be held regularly, and though some of the Federalists absented themselves rather pointedly, the president's supporters rallied to fill the gaps. During a time of stress and personal enmity, Dolley's good manners and good nature seemed to steady the Ship of State, as well as to uphold the harassed president in what private life was left to him.

His second inaugural, in March, 1813, was celebrated by all the usual ceremonies, though the president seemed to one observer tired and pale, exhausted by the repeated bowing from the waist which in those days took the place of handshaking.

Dolley and James Madison. Both painted by Gilbert Stuart in 1804 (Courtesy of the Pennsylvania Academy of the Fine Arts, above; Courtesy of Amherst College, below)

*Scotchtown, girlhood home of Dolley Madison
(The Valentine Museum, Richmond, Virginia)*

*The Green Room of the White House,
furnished in the Federal style of about 1800.
The portrait of Benjamin Franklin over the
mantel was painted by David Martin in 1767
(White House Historical Association)*

This portrait of George Washington by Gilbert Stuart survived the fire of 1814 and is now in the East Room of the White House (White House Historical Association)

John Adams, second president of the United States. Portrait by Gilbert Stuart (Courtesy of the New York Historical Society, New York City)

The Capitol Building before the fire of 1814, showing, between the two wings, the wooden walkway that was the first thing to go up in flames. Watercolor by Benjamin Latrobe (Library of Congress)

*After the fire of 1814 the White House was gutted,
and its outer walls were blackened by smoke
(White House Historical Association)*

A Gilbert Stuart portrait of Thomas Jefferson, who succeeded
John Adams as president. Jefferson designed and built
Monticello, his home near Charlottesville, Virginia (Above,
Bowdoin College Museum of Art; below, Courtesy of the
Thomas Jefferson Memorial Foundation)

ADMIRAL COCKBURN BURNING &
on the 1st of June 1813. done from a Ske

1. *Cockburn.*
2. *Westfall 1st Lieut of the Marlborough*
3. *Wayburn Capt of Marines.*
4. *Lieut Carter.*

UNDERING HAVRE DE GRACE
ken on the Spot at the time .

5. *Machine for throwing Rockets.*
6. *A New Coach part of the Plunder.*
7. *Mrs. Sears Tavern.*

*John Quincy Adams,
the sixth president of the
United States. Portrait
by Asher Durand
(Courtesy of the New
York Historical Society,
New York City)*

*James Monroe was
secretary of state under
Madison and succeeded
him in the presidency.
Portrait by John
Vanderlyn (White
House Historical
Association)*

Andrew Jackson, the first frontier-born president, presented a sharp contrast to the men who had served before him. Portrait by John Vanderlyn (Courtesy of the New York Historical Society, New York City)

When Dolley returned to Washington in 1837, she found that fashions had changed: at left, the Empire style that Dolley had worn as First Lady; at right, the newer costume of the 1830s.

Dolley Madison in later life.
Portrait by John Wood
(Library of Congress)

Montpellier, the house in Virginia where Dolley
and James Madison spent their summers and to which
they retired after 1817 (Library of Congress)

The White House in 1831 (White House Historical Association)

11

"Mr. Madison's War"

In the summer of 1813 Madison was attacked by the dread Potomac malaria, which carried with it a high fever and other symptoms so serious that it was said "his life hung on his nursing." Dolley never left that to anyone else, and gave him the most devoted care, cheerful, competent, and comforting, hiding from him her alarm and fatigue.

Those were days of tension and uncertainty in the nation's capital. The city of Washington itself had no military or strategic importance. It lay in the Y formed by the union of the Potomac and the Anacostia rivers, or the Eastern Branch as the latter was called, with a creek known as the Tiber flowing westward along the base of Capitol Hill through a marshy woodland. Alexandria, eight miles down the Potomac, was a much better and long established seaport. People inclined to whistle in the dark were mistakenly convinced that invasion by the British, if it came, would start at Boston, where the Federalist majority would welcome and possibly aid the enemy. Instead, Admiral Sir George Cockburn (which rhymed with "go-burn") brought his ships boldly into Chesapeake Bay, from where British officers in thin disguises were able to circulate in the streets and taverns. These smartly clad and reckless visitors were sometimes even entertained by stubbornly disaffected Americans, even while villages and farms along the shore were being raided for supplies, and burned for resisting the British foraging parties. They also had every opportunity to buy American newspapers and hire spies to report American preparations for defense, or the lack of them.

Dolley was almost alone during this frightening time, while her husband lay dangerously ill, and the British menaced the city. Madison's secretary, Edward Coles, who was always her mainstay, was absent in Philadelphia, also ill, and her son Payne Todd, now twenty years old, had been sent abroad to further his education.

"And now if I could I would describe to you the fears and alarms that circulate around me," Dolley wrote to Coles in May. "For the last week all the city and Georgetown (except the Cabinet) have expected a visit from the enemy, and were not lacking in their expressions of terror and reproach. We are making considerable efforts for defense. The Fort is being repaired, and five hundred militia, with perhaps as many regulars, are to be stationed on the Green near the windmill. The twenty tents already look well in my eyes, who have always been an advocate for fighting when assailed though a Quaker. I therefore keep the old Tunisia sabre within reach."

It appears that the intrepid Dolley would have placed herself at her husband's bedside to defend him with some trophy of the Algerian pirate wars.

"One of our generals has discovered a plan of the British," she continued, "to land as many chosen rogues as they can about fourteen miles below Alexandria in the night, so that they may be on hand to burn the President's house and offices. I do not tremble at this, but feel hurt that the Admiral (of

Havre de Grace memory) should send me word that he would make his bow at my drawing-room very soon. . . . Mr. Monroe and his family dined with us yesterday in a large party. Mr. Hay is with them, having come to escort Mrs. Monroe to Richmond on a visit to her two daughters."

Nothing was allowed to interfere with hospitality.

The reference to Havre de Grace, a small town in Maryland at the head of the bay, where the Susquehanna flows into it, arose from the most notorious raid yet perpetrated by Admiral Cockburn's men. The admiral himself had taken part in this outrage, to the extent of carrying off a handsome coach valued at $1000, in which he intended to ride through Washington after he had captured the city, and a sofa which caught his fancy for his shipboard cabin. His seamen roamed at will through the helpless town, appropriating furniture, silver, and horses, before setting fire to the houses and stables. Most of the local militia were absent at their rural homes in a false security, and Havre de Grace was pillaged and burned until even the British officers under Cockburn's command remonstrated. It was here that "the rockets' red glare" was first seen in America, adding to the terror of the inhabitants. The rocket was a recent invention, a projectile with an iron head which could be charged with grapeshot or fire-making materials. It had very little aim, and simply destroyed at random, and it would soon be abandoned when the accuracy of artillery fire was improved to surpass it.

Baltimore, which lay where the Patapsco River emptied into the bay below Havre de Grace, was known to be well defended, and had set up relays of mounted couriers to carry the alarm, and the British left it alone. Washington itself was guarded—after a fashion—by the unfinished Fort Warburton, later called Fort Washington, on the east shore of the Potomac below Alexandria. Fire from the guns at the fort would have raked any enemy ship coming up the bay towards the capital, and earthworks were being thrown up along the water front.

"We have been in a state of perturbation here for a long time," Dolley wrote to Edward Coles from the White House. "The depredations of the enemy approaching within twenty miles of the city and the disaffected [Americans] making incessant difficulties for the Government. Such a place as this has become! I cannot describe it. I wish for my part that we were in Philadelphia. The people here do not deserve that I should prefer Washington. Among the other exclamations and threats, they say that if Mr. Madison attempts to move from this house in case of an attack they will stop him and that he shall *fall with it!* I am determined to stay with him. Our preparations for defense, by some means or other, are constantly retarded; but the small force the British have in the Bay will never venture nearer than at present, twenty-three miles."

The expected attack did not come then, for the British fleet fell back down the bay to attack Norfolk and Hampton at the mouth of the James River. There Cockburn's men acted with even greater brutality than at Havre de Grace, on the word of a British officer named Napier, whose diary recorded that "every act of rapine and plunder was encouraged," and the women trapped in the captured towns suffered rape and gunshot wounds. Cockburn was a noisy swaggerer, brutal even by the rough standards of the navy of his day, and his name was now detested throughout America. He settled down for the winter of 1813–14 at a house on the Georgia coast, from where he threatened to liberate and arm the slaves against their masters.

By the time Madison was convalescent, Washington was no longer directly menaced, and he took up his burden of work again, while Dolley resumed her social program to show that no one was nervous, and to help maintain the morale of the city.

"I have the happiness to assure you that Mr. Madison is recovering," she wrote to Coles early in July. "For the last three weeks his fever has been so slight as to permit him to take bark [quinine] every hour, with good effect. It is three months now that I have nursed him, night and day—sometimes with despair. But now that I see that he will get well, I feel as if I might die myself from fatigue!"

Cockburn's departure from the bay so relieved the citizens of Washington that the capital became excessively gay, with weddings, dinner parties, dancing assemblies, the formal glitter and pomp of the embassy entertainments, and balls at the Navy Yard where the newly imported waltz was introduced as the latest sensation. The city was full of personable young men in uniform, and the society belles did not lack for beaux. "Fringe parties" became the fashion, where the young ladies made with their own fine needlework the epaulets for the officers' uniforms.

A New Year's Day reception at the White House was now an established custom, and in 1814 it was quite as brilliant as in happier times. But there was a dark undercurrent of apprehension, and a Washington matron wrote that "a plan might be carried into execution, without a miracle, of seizing the President and Secretaries with only fifty or a hundred men, and rendering this nation a laughing-stock to every other in the world. I did not think much of these possibilities until hearing them discussed by General Van Ness and others, who, far from wishing a parade of guards or ridiculous apprehension to be entertained, were yet anxious that the city should not be unprepared for a danger which certainly did exist."

It was about this time that young Elbridge Gerry, son of the vice-president, recorded in his diary his valuable impressions of the White House, which was soon to be obliterated by fire:

"The President's house is a perfect palace. You enter the

front door and are at once in a large hall, which is as an entry, etc. Pillars of immense size are dispersed through this; and it is handsomely furnished, etc., and has large lamps for the whole length. On the side opposite to the entrance are doors opening to four rooms. The corner is the dining-room and is very spacious and twice the height of modern parlors and three times as large. This is furnished in the most elegant manner, and the furniture is so large that, as Mrs. Cutts says, the sideboard would cover the whole side of a large parlor. At the head of the room, General Washington is represented as large as life. This room opens by a single door into Mrs. Madison's sitting-room, which is half as large. This is furnished equally as well, and has more elegant and delicate furniture. Her portrait is here seen. This room, in the same way, enters into the drawing-room which is an immense and magnificent room in oval form, and which form is preserved in those above and even to the cellar. A door opens at each end, one into the hall, and the opposite one into the terrace, from whence you have an excellent view of all the rivers, etc. The windows are nearly the height of the room, and have superb red velvet curtains which cost $4.00 a yard. The chairs are wood-painted, with worked bottoms, and each has a red velvet cushion. They are arranged on the side, and are divided into four divisions by sofas. These three rooms are all open on levee nights."

At a Cabinet meeting in the past July Madison had placed the defense of the capital in the hands of General John Armstrong, who was secretary of war, and General William Winder, a debonair Maryland lawyer with little military experience. Armstrong had fought as a young man in the army of the Revolution, and since then had failed to distinguish himself in the Canadian campaign of 1812. Winder had also taken part in the Canadian disaster, and had spent some time as a prisoner at Quebec. Both men proved to be a bad choice, but

Madison had very little to choose from at the time, and was no soldier himself. Most of the Revolutionary War heroes were aged or dead, and there was no precedent for the situation in which Madison found himself; one with which Washington could have dealt decisively, and probably with success. A personal hostility between Armstrong and Secretary of State Monroe, and Armstrong's expressed desire to see an end to "the Virginia Dynasty" in Government was a serious complication. Monroe met Armstrong's gruff bad manners with an icy courtesy. The amiable Winder had few qualifications for organizing an army and a staff.

Meanwhile a British army from the Peninsular War in Spain had been freed from combat by Bonaparte's abdication, and could be dispatched to America by Wellington under the command of General Robert Ross, an able, disciplined, professional soldier. These experienced troops were joined by others at Bermuda, and another British squadron of frigates under Admiral Cochrane arrived there to transport Ross's force to the American seaboard. On August 17, 1814, the ships passed by the Potomac and reached the mouth of the Patuxent River, the next waterway of any size opening into the Chesapeake Bay north of the Potomac. Marines and Ross's veteran Line regiments began landing the next day at the little town of Benedict in Maryland, which was as far up the river as the transports could go, and only about thirty miles overland from Washington. At the same time Cockburn returned to the Chesapeake with his marines and began committing new outrages on the Virginia shore of the Potomac.

Ross, having served under Wellington's discipline in Spain, forbade pillage and maintained order around Benedict, in contrast to Cockburn's plundering habits. Ross had no animals, so the men dragged the big guns ashore by long ropes. They found the town of Benedict deserted by its inhabitants—

because of Havre de Grace—and the troops met no resistance as under a blistering August sun they established a camp on shore and began to form their brigades in preparation for their march towards the capital. On the morning of August 18 a foaming horse brought a messenger to Washington from Point Lookout at the mouth of the Potomac, to inform the astonished War Department that the British were north and east of Washington and were landing an army in Maryland and not from the Potomac side as might have been expected.

Calm as Dolley had contrived to remain, after the shocking news of the landing at Benedict became known in Washington the city went into panic. Everyone thronged into the streets or began to collect their most precious household goods for flight. Couriers on sweating horses rode out to urge the state governors to summon the unwilling militia, most of which never appeared. Stories of the horrors at Havre de Grace and Norfolk were revived, and induced many men of substance to send their women and children westward across Rock Creek to Georgetown and even beyond, to Frederick in the western Maryland hills. Rumors of the size of the invading force were exaggerated, and the dusty roads west and north of the capital soon were crowded with refugees who had heard of Cockburn's methods in an occupied town. The horse-drawn stages setting out for New York and Boston were filled with frightened passengers who spread the alarm as they went. To Dolley, who could remember when yellow fever had emptied the city of Philadelphia in 1793, the scenes of disorder and heedless flight were hideously familiar. Plague or war. War or plague. It was the same.

The Cabinet, an island of false calm, conferred at the White House while the enemy disposed itself in leisurely professional style for its march on the capital. Monroe's experience of Revolutionary days, when he had fought in General Washington's army at Trenton and Princeton, caused him to offer to mount a horse himself and ride out with a small escort towards the British camp at Benedict to reconnoitre, and Madison gratefully agreed. Thus it was that a Cabinet member with no military rank became a volunteer scout on horseback, in place of the commanding officer or the secretary of war, whose business it conceivably was. Winder was active enough in his showy way, rushing about on horseback to oversee the local defenses instead of sitting down to plan an organized campaign to beat off the invading army. Under his direction, earthworks dating from the Havre de Grace alarm two years before were repaired and extended.

The District of Columbia militia were ordered to mobilize at the foot of Capitol Hill on the night of the nineteenth under Winder's command. Many of them reported for duty without guns, uniforms, or military equipment of any kind, and they were sent away again to provide themselves with weapons, "if only with butcher knives." By Saturday morning, the twentieth, when Monroe from behind the screen of a pine forest was observing Ross's men around Benedict, some militia had again assembled in Washington city, and they presented an encouraging sight to the obstinate optimists who wrote for the newspapers, and the valiant women who like Dolley were determined to stay with their men in the city.

Nevertheless, the banks prepared to move their cash inland, and the State Department clerks began to fill large linen bags with their files and records, while Armstrong from his office in the same building remarked that these precautions looked to him "like unnecessary alarm." Wagons which should have carried rations to the military camp which Winder had established at a place called Woodyard in Maryland, between Washington and Benedict, were commandeered to transport government papers across the Potomac into Virginia, where they were placed under guard in an unoccupied house in Leesburg. Otherwise, many valuable Revolutionary documents, congressional records and secret journals, George Washington's commission and wartime correspondence, laws, treaties, and diplomatic records, all would have perished.

Armstrong remained paralyzed by his own unfounded conviction that the British had no intention of coming to Washington. What, he would inquire blandly, could they want with Washington when Baltimore was nearby, a valuable port and a full-grown, flourishing city worth taking? But Baltimore had its defenses. And Washington was the capital. He could not see the difference.

Winder was calling frantically for volunteers, but few responded. Monroe arrived at Winder's camp at Woodyard, and his despatches from there to the president told of the advance in a marching column of about 4,000 red-coated British regulars towards Bladensburg, on the very doorstep of Washington. It was a small Maryland town just outside the District of Columbia line, whose main street ended in a bridge over the Eastern Branch, where a road leading into Washington began. The decision was taken to defend this bridge, which lay only six miles from the eastern edge of the capital. It occurred to no one in command that it would have been far simpler to blow it up at once and form defense lines behind its ruins.

On Monday the twenty-second Madison collected a small party including Armstrong, Secretary of the Navy William Jones, and Attorney General Richard Rush, son of the famous Philadelphia doctor. With them he rode out across the Navy Yard bridge into Maryland. There was some idea that the presence among them of the president himself might encourage the throng of ill-fed, disorganized militia, volunteers, sailors, and soldiers, who sent up a ragged, half-hearted cheer when he was recognized. He spent that night at Winder's camp, which was said to resemble "a race-course or a fair" more than a military base, and he reviewed the straggling ranks of the makeshift army the next morning. It was now believed that the British, who had advanced as far as Upper Marlborough, would first try to seize Annapolis as a base for their operations to attack either Baltimore or Washington. This foolish guess seemed to allow plenty of time for the Americans to assemble and position their untrained forces. When Madison left the Woodyard camp about 2 P.M. to return to Washington with Armstrong, Rush, and their small escort, they did not know that Ross was already marching from Upper Marlborough and was then only three miles behind them.

When Winder discovered that the British were actually on the move towards him, he made a running retreat into Washington with his men, and set up a temporary camp near the Navy Yard. He then showed up at the White House to explain that he had feared a night attack on his unprepared army, and had thought best to remove it from Ross's path. He had however divided his forces in order to leave about 2500 men under General Tobias Stansbury of Maryland to defend the bridge at Bladensburg. His own men were exhausted from the hasty retreat in intense August heat, a temperature which even the hardened British were unaccustomed to, so that many of them also had dropped in their tracks.

Monroe remained with Stansbury's militia at Bladensburg—he had hardly been out of the saddle for three days. At midnight of the twenty-third, a scribbled note from him was delivered at the White House: "The enemy are in full march for Washington. Have the materials prepared to destroy the bridges. You had better remove the records." This was advice which should have come from the secretary of war, but the secretary of state was the better soldier.

The last night the Madisons were to spend at the White House was a sleepless one.

12

The Burning
of Washington

At 11 A.M. on Wednesday the twenty-fourth, Armstrong was still dithering around in Washington when Winder reluctantly moved his men out from his Navy Yard camp to a point at Old Fields (now Forestville, Maryland) several miles nearer Washington than his deserted position at Woodyard, which had been occupied by the British bivouac the night before. From Old Fields he intended to support Stansbury at Bladensburg. Madison ordered Armstrong to follow him with militia which had so far remained idle at Washington, and this removed from the city its last defenders visible to the inhabitants.

An hour later the president, with a brace of borrowed dueling pistols buckled around his waist, rode out after them with three companions, one of whom was the faithful Rush. He left Dolley in the White House surrounded by her terrified but loyal servants.

The heat was oppressive that day, as only Potomac heat can be, and a rumor ran through the streets that the water supply had been poisoned. Dolley hurried from room to room, gathering the presidential silver, the best clocks and ornaments, and those of Madison's treasured books and papers which she considered it essential to preserve. A letter from her to Anna Cutts, begun on Tuesday and finished the next day, gives a vivid picture of what she went through while awaiting further news from her husband:

"DEAR SISTER—My husband left me yesterday morning to join General Winder. He inquired anxiously whether I had courage or firmness to remain in the President's House until his return on the morrow, or succeeding day, and on my assurance that I had no fear but for him and the success of our army, he left, beseeching me to take care of myself, and of the Cabinet papers, public and private. I have since received two despatches from him, written with a pencil. The last is alarming, because he desires I should be ready at a moment's warning to enter my carriage and leave the city; that the enemy seemed stronger than had at first been reported, and it might happen that they would reach the city with the intention of destroying it. I am accordingly ready; I have pressed as many Cabinet papers into trunks as to fill one carriage; our private property must be sacrificed, as it is impossible to procure wagons for its transportation. I am determined not to go myself until I see Mr. Madison safe, so that he can accompany me, as I hear of much hostility towards him.

"Disaffection stalks around us. My friends and acquaintances are all gone, even Colonel C.[arroll] with his hundred men who were stationed as a guard in this enclosure. French John [Sioussat] with his usual activity and resolution offers to spike the cannon at the gate and lay a train of powder which would blow up the British, should they enter the house. To the last proposition I positively object, without being able to make him understand why all advantages in war may not be taken.

"*Wednesday morning, twelve o'clock.*—Since sunrise I have been turning my spy-glass in every direction, and watching with unwearied anxiety, hoping to discover the approach of my dear husband and his friends; but alas! I can descry only groups of military, wandering in all directions, as if there was a lack of arms, or of spirit to fight for their own firesides.

"*Three o'clock.*—Will you believe it, my sister? we have had a battle, or skirmish, near Bladensburg, and here I am still, within sound of the cannon! Mr. Madison comes not. May God protect us! Two messengers, covered with dust, come to bid me fly; but here I mean to wait for him. . . . At this late hour a wagon has been procured, and I have had it filled with plate and the most valuable portable articles belonging to the house. Whether it will reach its destination, the Bank of Maryland, or fall into the hands of British soldiery, events must determine. Our kind friend Mr. Carroll has come to hasten my departure, and in a very bad humor with me because I insist on waiting until the large picture of General Washington is secured, and it requires to be unscrewed from the wall. This process was found too tedious for those perilous moments; I have ordered the frame to be broken, and the canvas taken out. It is done! and the precious portrait is placed in the hands of two gentlemen of New York for safe keeping. And now, dear sister, I must leave this house, or the retreating army will make me a prisoner in it by filling up the road I am to take. When I shall write again to you, or where I shall be tomorrow, I cannot tell! DOLLEY."

The devoted French steward, Jean Sioussat, was the last to leave the White House, after he had seen Dolley off safely in her carriage, accompanied by her faithful maid Sukey and followed by the wagonload of portable valuables he had helped her to assemble. She left behind her expensive wardrobe and her personal belongings, imported turbans, footwear, and other

treasures of her own, in order to make room in the wagon for
what she considered national property. Sioussat carried her pet
macaw to the house of a friend before locking the doors of the
White House and depositing the key with the French minister, whose flag would be respected by the invaders.

Following the president along the road towards Winder's
camp below Bladensburg, we find him with Monroe, from
whom he learned that the British, having spent the night at
Woodyard, were just entering the town of Bladensburg from
the opposite direction. Winder and Armstrong were nowhere
to be seen, but Winder's men had been joined to Stansbury's
so that a semblance of resistance at the bridge was thought
possible. There was no leadership and no discipline among the
raw American force, which resulted in a conflict of orders,
and a lack of confidence naturally prevailed.

Ignorant of the exact location and extent of the American
position, Madison and Rush rode through the militia lines and
out the other side, until they were warned by a scout that they
had come within gunshot of the British, who were approaching just over the hill, and that the president was in danger of
being taken prisoner. They turned back in some haste and
encountered Armstrong, Winder, and Monroe, who urged
Madison to return to Washington at once. The British had
begun letting off their terrifying rockets, some of which fell
and exploded nearby. The noise and flash of these unaimed
missiles created panic among the militia and the mob of civil-
ian spectators who had rashly come out from Washington to
see the battle. The result was a general stampede back towards
the city, while Ross led his red column across the Bladensburg
bridge, taking heavy casualties from hidden artillery on the
American side. His seasoned troops stood the fire, and set up
their skirmish lines on the west, or Washington bank of the
river, while the Americans deserted their guns and fled. This

"battle" was later derisively known as "the Bladensburg Races."

Both Armstrong and Winder arrived at Capitol Hill in Washington ahead of their troops—they had horses—and Monroe joined them there while the retreating militia flowed past them towards Georgetown, sometimes stopping to steal food and loot along the way. Nobody knew where the president was by now, but he was thought to be at the White House.

Meanwhile, Colonel Charles Carroll had finally prevailed upon Dolley, almost by force, to allow herself to be removed from in front of the British army. If she had been caught there she would have suffered indignities if not actual danger when the city was occupied by the enemy. Her capture would have supplied the British with a powerful advantage and caused her husband untold anguish and humiliation. It had been arranged that she should await him at Carroll's house called Bellevue in Georgetown, where the family of Secretary of the Navy Jones had already taken refuge.

The record of the ensuing days and the whereabouts of the Madisons is still obscure, and many picturesque legends have grown up around their adventures while the British were in possession of Washington. It appears that Madison reached the White House only minutes after she had left it, and was persuaded by Rush and Colonel John Mason, who never left his side, that she was in safe hands and that he must at all costs save himself from capture. He rode with them to a tavern at Falls Church in Virginia, west and south of Washington, and from there to Salona, the home of the Reverend William Maffitt, where he spent the night, hoping that Dolley would be brought to him. But in the hurry and confusion, messages miscarried or were never sent, and unknown to him Dolley was only a mile or so away at Rokeby, the home of her friend Mrs.

Matilda Lee Love. Mrs. Love recorded that "a number of city people took refuge at my house the night the British took Washington. Mr. Madison had gone further up the country. Early in the evening Mr. Monroe came to my house to look for Mr. Madison; as Mr. Monroe was so weary I gave him his supper and asked him if he thought I was safe where I was for the night. 'Madam,' he said, 'as safe as if you were in the Allegheny Mountains.' "

And so she was, but Mr. Monroe took a good deal upon himself to say so. None of them knew that the president was only a few minutes' ride away, at Salona.

The British entered Washington down Maryland Avenue at twilight on August 24, 1814, to find most of the houses closed and deserted, and the streets almost empty. The infamous Admiral Cockburn rode in beside Ross, urging him to burn the city to the ground, which went against Ross's disciplined inclination. As they came into sight of the Capitol at the end of Maryland Avenue, a single volley was fired from a house at the corner of 2nd Street. It struck Ross's horse, which fell dead beneath him.

A search of the house proved it to be deserted and no guns were found, but the triumphal entry had been marred and Ross gave the order for the house to be burned. That was the first fire set by the British that day.

Ross led his troops—an advance guard of about 200 men to take possession of a national capital—to an open field east of the Capitol Building, about where the Library of Congress now stands, and a rough camp was established there. No one appeared with the authority to negotiate with him for the surrender of the city. Cockburn was roaring destruction and hellfire, and Ross—still unable to believe in so easy a conquest—took a detachment of soldiers to the Capitol as darkness fell. His men fired into the windows, shattering the glass, but there was no sign of life within. The locks were then shot off the doors and the two wings were searched for sharpshooters. None was found, but kegs of gunpowder were set in the wooden passage or ropewalk connecting the two legislative chambers—the Rotunda had not yet been built to link them—and when the powder exploded into fire the troops piled up books and papers and broken furniture along with some tar barrels in the House and Senate chambers and kindled them too. The old shingle roof caught rapidly, and the wooden floors fed the blaze, which burned so fiercely that some of the marble columns cracked and crumbled in the heat.

Ross and Cockburn gathered their men to proceed down Pennsylvania Avenue towards the White House. In the oncoming darkness lit by the blazing Capitol the Navy Yard was seen to be also in flames, set by its own commandant in retreat under orders from Navy Secretary Jones, to prevent the British from seizing the ammunition, stores, and equipment there.

The British march by torchlight down tree-shadowed Pennsylvania Avenue was a parade without drumbeat or bugle, and even the tramp of the soldiers' feet was muffled by the deep dust of the roadway. The few houses along the way were dark, shuttered, and empty. Arrived at the White House, the troops with Cockburn's approval broke open the door and roamed through the rooms, smashing or carrying off whatever caught their eye. The admiral himself took a cushion from what he assumed was Mrs. Madison's chair, with a few vulgar remarks, and encouraged the men to help themselves to Madison's fine cellar of wines and the provisions with which the mansion was stocked.

The French minister, Sérurier, who remained in Washington throughout the invasion, protected by his flag, recorded that as his house was near the president's he feared for its safety when he saw British soldiers approaching with lighted torches. He hastened out to ask for a guard to be placed around his residence, and found Ross in the oval drawing room where the president's househood goods were being gathered in a pile to be burned. His request for protection was granted, with Ross's compliments.

About midnight, when everything of any value had been confiscated into the soldiers' knapsacks and pockets, or destroyed by their gun-butts, and the cellar and larder had been emptied, they went from room to room with their torches, setting fire to the draperies at the windows and whatever could be tossed into piles to feed the blaze. All Dolley's new furniture, all her fine yellow damask and red velvet and imported rugs and crystal chandeliers, her gowns and headdresses left in the cupboards, and many of Madison's valuable books, were consumed, as the flames burst through the broken windows and licked up the outside of the house.

Ross and Cockburn then made their way to a tavern near the Treasury Building and ordered supper from the frightened landlady, and ate it by the light of the conflagration. They spent the night in a house in Carroll Row east of the Capitol, whose owner was forced to give them hospitality. All that night the sky over Washington glowed red from the holocaust, which was visible to the Madisons from their separate refuges, appearing to be much worse than it was, for private property had been respected by Ross except for those houses suspected of concealing snipers.

The next morning, in the humid August heat and fitful winds which precede a tropical storm, the invaders rekindled their smoldering fire at the Treasury Building, set the State and War Department Building blazing, and burned the offices of the *National Intelligencer* newspaper, whose editorials had long offended them.

That same morning Madison rode back to the tavern at Falls Church, hoping to find his wife there, but returned to Salona without her. The fires still burned in Washington under a black pall of smoke which hung on the heavy air. But in the afternoon of the twenty-fifth a sudden hurricane swept in over the city, bringing torrential rains which gradually quenched the flames its high winds had fanned.

Ross was aware by now that outraged American forces were rallying in the countryside, lacking only leadership, and he was a long way from his ships. He had decided to withdraw to Benedict on the night of the twenty-fifth, but before he could do so the storm struck the city, forcing everyone to take what shelter he could find. A British account said that "the most tremendous hurricane ever remembered by the inhabitants broke over Washington the day after the conflagration. Roofs of houses were torn off and carried into the air like sheets of paper, while the rain that accompanied it was like the rushing of a cataract. This lasted for two hours without intermission, during which many of the houses spared by us were blown down, and thirty of our men and as many more of the inhabitants were buried beneath their ruins. Two cannons standing upon a bit of rising ground were fairly lifted up into the air and carried several yards to the rear."

The British camp in the field on Capitol Hill was a shambles of soaked tents, provisions, and equipment, much of which was blown away entirely. After the storm had finally abated about 9 P.M. the last British pickets were called in and the retreat began, back across Bladensburg battlefield, where many of the dead and wounded still lay, and on through Upper Marlborough, till they reached the landing place on the Patuxent. They had occupied Washington almost exactly twenty-four hours.

13

Reunion

The storm was of course providential, as it put out the fires and discouraged further marauding by the British. It also caught a multitude of homeless refugees on the roads and drenched their poor possessions they had thought to save by flight. It overtook Madison on his way from Salona to Wiley's Tavern near Great Falls, where he had at last learned that Dolley had gone with the Jones family in the hope of finding him.

He took refuge from the hurricane at a house along the way, and then resumed his journey, to be reunited with his distracted wife at Wiley's. The men of the party discussed taking the women and children on to Frederick for safety, but changed their minds when a muddy courier arrived with the news that the British were evacuating Washington and drawing back towards their ships at Benedict. Madison thought it was his duty to return to the capital at once. Dolley was to remain at Wiley's until he sent her word that it was safe for her to join him.

He was sixty-three years old, and always in frail health, and he had been on horseback most of the time for four days in a state of acute anxiety. But so far from the accusation that he had fled from Washington thinking only of his own safety, he had recognized the necessity of preventing the capture of the American president by the enemy, and provided in every possible way for the safety of others in his party before setting out again almost alone to the ravaged city.

He accumulated a sizable escort as he went, and the word of his intention was passed ahead of him. Riding roundabout from Montgomery Courthouse—from where a small force of reassembled militia had just set out for Baltimore with Winder—he spent the night of the twenty-sixth at the home of Mrs. Henrietta Bentley in the little Quaker village of Brookeville. Mrs. Smith, who always got the news, was able to describe the scene at the Bentley house as it was reported to her by her daughters, who were there.

"Just at bed-time the President arrived, and all hands went to work to prepare supper and lodgings for him, his companions, and guards. Beds were spread in the parlor, as the house was filled, and guards were placed round the house during the night. . . . The fires they kindled and the lights within the tents had a beautiful appearance. All the villagers, gentlemen and ladies, young and old, thronged to see the President. He was tranquil as usual, and though much distressed by the dreadful event which had taken place, was not dispirited."

Madison sent off express riders that night to summon Monroe from an army bivouac and Armstrong from his Frederick refuge, requesting them to meet him in Washington. The next morning he sent word to Dolley that the enemy were retreating on board their ships, and that he and Rush—his faithful companion still—were leaving at once for Washington. "You will of course take the same resolution," he added, with full confidence in her courage and devotion. "I know not where we are to hide our heads, but shall look for a place on my arrival. Mr. Rush offers us his house in the Six Buildings. Perhaps I may fall in with Mr. Cutts and have the benefit of his advice."

The Cutts family had taken over the house in F Street, and Madison knew they would be welcome there. He was not yet fully aware that everything he and Dolley had in the world, except Montpellier, had been reduced to ashes.

Madison and Monroe reached the devastated capital about five o'clock on the afternoon of the twenty-seventh. The British had departed in such haste that they had left about a hundred of their wounded behind them at a makeshift hospital in Carroll Row. A citizens' committee had buried nearly as many British dead. General Winder, arriving outside Baltimore with a small force, estimated the American dead at about two hundred.

The president's party had not been long at Rush's house when a thunder of cannon began down the river, seeming to indicate a naval attack on Fort Washington from the Potomac after all. The fort was at once blown up and deserted by its defenders, and a British detachment of frigates and rocket ships under Captain James Gordon in the *Seahorse* proceeded unhindered towards Alexandria. Early on the morning of the twenty-ninth they were plundering the wharves and warehouses of an undefended city.

In the absence of both Winder and Armstrong, the president asked Monroe to take charge at Washington. Madison with some members of his Cabinet rode out to inspect the damage in the city and plan a defense against a possible new invasion from the Potomac. The Cutts family had returned from their Maryland refuge to the house on F Street, and the President paused there to write a note to Dolley. He advised her to remain at Wiley's till further notice, as a landing by the British from the river below Washington would only force her to flee again. But by the time he returned to the house after a tour of inspection at the ruined Navy Yard, Dolley had already arrived there. She had set out at once on receiving his letter from Brookeville.

The Cutts house became temporary presidential headquarters and a guard was set up around it. Mrs. Thornton still lived next door, and with Mrs. Smith she called on Dolley that evening to exchange adventures, for they had remained in Washington and witnessed the brief British occupation.

The ease with which Alexandria had succumbed led to the expectation that Georgetown might be next, and the Baltimore defenses also were being strengthened. Its harbor was protected by Fort McHenry at the mouth of the Patapsco River, but Ross had given out his intention of setting up his winter headquarters in the prosperous city.

In Washington public opinion had swung round to support Madison, though there were still some people who laid the blame for Washington's inadequate defense on his shoulders, and there had been various threats against him, so that his casual presence among the troops and citizens at work repairing the waterfront defenses at Georgetown caused some concern for his personal safety. But when Secretary of War Armstrong finally appeared there, he was openly denounced for his witless conduct at the time of the Benedict landing. Charles Carroll, who encountered him at the new fortifications, loudly refused to take his proffered hand, and there was a general resolve not to serve under his orders again. A message to the president was composed to say "that every officer would tear off his epaulets if General Armstrong was to have anything to do with them." This was delivered to Madison as he was riding back to F Street with Rush and another companion. He read it with his usual calm deliberation, and returned the answer that "the contingency [of Armstrong remaining in command] shall not happen." Armstrong resigned, at the president's request, protesting that the criticism of him was inspired by intrigue and falsehood. Madison felt his own responsibilities very keenly as chief executive and commander in chief, and realized too late that the secretary of war should have been dismissed as soon as what Madison later called "his objectionable peculiarities" became obvious at the time of the Benedict landing.

Both the Capitol and the White House, at opposite ends of Pennsylvania Avenue, were fire-gutted, smoke-blackened ruins, whose outer walls still stood, but many private residences were unharmed. A temporary government was set up in the Patent Office on F Street between 8th and 9th, which had been spared by the British torches, though the building was damaged by the hurricane.

The first impression that Washington as a city had been wiped out by the fire prevailed for several days until it was discovered gradually that the chief harm was to the main public buildings. Mrs. Smith took a dreary view of things: "Already in one night have hundreds of our citizens been reduced from affluence to poverty, for it is not to be expected that Washington will ever again be the seat of Government," she wrote. Philadelphia rose to the occasion with an urgent invitation for the government to establish itself there, where many people had always thought it belonged.

But Madison and Monroe were already at work, Monroe combining in his single efficient person the offices of secretary of state and acting secretary of war. The government departments whose quarters had been destroyed by fire settled into cramped quarters in whatever private houses were available for rent, the banks reopened for business, and entertaining by the habitual hostesses began to revive—the chief topic of conversation being rival tales of horror and presence of mind during the occupation experience.

In the general exodus from Washington when the British first landed at Benedict, the French minister Sérurier, whose diplomatic immunity proved very useful to his friends, had been persuaded by the Tayloe family [of Mount Airy, Virginia] to give the protection of his flag to their beautiful Washington residence known as the Octagon House. This handsome dwelling stood on New York Avenue at 18th Street, and had been built about 1798, regardless of expense, after one of Thornton's finest designs. Sérurier had established the French Embassy there, and he now offered the undamaged house to the president, as a more roomy and convenient executive residence than F Street. The offer was gratefully accepted, with Colonel Tayloe's approval. With the various departments scattered about in whatever temporary accommodations they could find, government business was resumed.

The British army was again aboard its ships and not badly hurt by its adventure in Washington, and there was considerable alarm as to where it would strike next. On September 11 word reached Washington by fast courier that fifty British vessels had arrived at the mouth of the Patapsco River fourteen miles below Baltimore. The city's defenses were organized under the competent General Samuel Smith, and the remnants of Winder's Bladensburg army had arrived there.

Hulks had been sunk below Fort McHenry to block the channel, and just in time. The British landed a force of some 9,000 soldiers and marines for an overland assault from North Point, where a road led into the city. They were met by Smith's militia who had marched out halfway the night before. General Ross was killed in the first skirmish, and there is a touching tradition that he had only time to speak his wife's name as he fell back into the arms of his aides. He died there, by the roadside. His men soon retreated to their ships, having discovered that the American militia could be effective if properly led. Admiral Cockburn had boasted that he would take Fort McHenry in a couple of hours, but it withstood twenty-five hours of steady bombardment from the river, even though its guns were outranged. During that long night of September 13, 1814, a young Maryland lawyer named Francis Scott Key stood at the rail of a ship offshore and watched "the rockets' red glare, the bombs bursting in air" over the fort, while the battered flag still flew. He had been sent under a white flag of truce with a companion to negotiate with Cochrane for the release of a well-known physician who had been taken prisoner at Upper Marlborough during the British retreat, and all three Americans were detained until daybreak lest they carry information ashore. Convinced of failure, the British finally put Key and his companions ashore and withdrew down the river. They had lost Ross, the American militia under Smith's leadership had stood their ground, and Fort McHenry had not surrendered.

By mid-October the British fleet had withdrawn from the Chesapeake entirely and sailed for Jamaica for repairs, taking the army with it. This move seemed to indicate that the next attack would be launched at New Orleans, for the control of the Mississippi.

14

"Mr. Madison's Peace"

When the year 1814 ended, the Congress was accommodated in a new brick building hastily constructed by public subscription as its temporary quarters. It stood on Capitol Hill, about where the Supreme Court Building is now, and ended all discussion of removing the government to another city, even during the reconstruction of the original Capitol Building. Congress held its sessions in this "little Capitol" from 1815 to 1819.

Latrobe was recalled to superintend the work on the ruins, and found that much of the materials could still be used in the reconstruction. In 1817 he turned the work over to Charles Bulfinch of Boston, who completed the building according to the plans of Latrobe and Thornton. To Bulfinch we owe the central Rotunda uniting the two wings, which had been joined only by the covered wooden walkway which was the first thing to go up in flames. Bulfinch also erected the first low dome. His work was not completed till 1828, and the Capitol since then has been enlarged and the dome has been altered and raised.

The greatest loss in the Capitol fire was the library then housed on the lower floor. Jefferson at Monticello was deeply grieved at its destruction, and offered his own personal library, lovingly collected during his years abroad and at home, and containing some ten thousand volumes, to replace it. Congress accepted this generous gesture, and valued Jefferson's treasured books at $24,000, though they were doubtless worth, even then, several times that amount. He was not a man to haggle. His daughters helped him to wrap and pack the books in boxes, which were hauled to Washington in ten wagon-loads, to form the nucleus of today's fine Congressional Library.

The original architect of the White House, James Hoban, was engaged to supervise the reconstruction of the gutted, roofless dwelling of the president, which the Madisons would not occupy again. Work began at once, for it was found that the outer walls were sound enough to remain as the shell of the new building, and the smoke-stained sandstone was finally given a coat of white paint, so that it was thereafter truly the White House.

Always adaptable and cheerful, Dolley settled into the Octagon House on New York Avenue, almost within sight of the first President's House, and resumed her social program of dinner parties and Wednesday night receptions. The Octagon House had actually six sides and not eight, and in its design Thornton had really let himself go in the classical style of the 18th-century Adam brothers. With unlimited money to spend, he had chosen to use imported brick for the exterior instead of the local sandstone. Even the window casings and glass were specially made in a curved form for the rounded rooms. A circular chamber above the ground floor vestibule became Madison's office, and the spacious drawing room on the main floor was a handsome setting for Dolley's entertaining. George Washington had seen and admired the house when it was new, but it had had an unhappy history in the possession of its builder and was said to be haunted. After a quarrel with her father about the man she was forbidden to marry, one of Colonel Tayloe's daughters had fallen to her death down the well of the graceful spiral staircase which wound upward to the third story from the circular entrance hall. Another daughter had tripped on the steps and broken her back. Understandably, Tayloe had abandoned the house and returned to Mount Airy. As a handsome curiosity it was turned over to Sérurier for its protection in the summer of 1814.

The New Year's Day reception there in 1815 was as gay and glittering as though there had been no war at all. Dolley must have had some shopping done for her in Philadelphia and New York, for there were no dressmakers' establishments in the village which Washington was then to provide the fashionable gowns she always appeared in, as though to show how little damage the British had been able to do to her accustomed way of life. Her costume for the 1815 reception was described by one of her feminine guests as rose-colored satin trimmed with ermine, a white satin turban with white ostrich plumes "fastened by a crescent," and gold ornaments for jewelry. The refreshments served at the Octagon House under Sioussat's direction were just as lavish as those which had been provided at the White House before war was declared. Secretary Coles returned to them that winter, and brought with him his sister Sally, for since Anna's marriage there was always a need in Dolley's heart and home for a sister of some kind to keep her company.

Meanwhile a peace commission, including John Quincy Adams and Senator Henry Clay, was negotiating with the British at Ghent. But the news of Andrew Jackson's victory over the British at New Orleans, which saved the Mississippi, arrived at Washington before the courier from Ghent brought the treaty which finally ended the War of 1812. Its reception on February 14 was dramatic. The Octagon House was brightly lighted that night as the citizens crowded in to celebrate and to congratulate the president on the victory. Somebody played "The President's March," the wine flowed freely, even in the servants' quarters, and Jean Sioussat permitted himself to get gloriously drunk, while people upstairs partook of the splendid refreshments and clasped each other's hands with tears of joy.

Later the treaty would be criticized for its shortcomings, of which Madison and his advisors were well aware when they gathered that night in the circular office to study its terms. At the same time they shrewdly realized that "the affair" at New Orleans was a better guarantee of peace than any parchment signed by the commissioners at Ghent could be. The Mississippi River had been secured for the United States, and England's interference with her one-time colonies was at an end.

In the general relief from the tensions and anxieties of the war years, 1815 burst into social gaiety, despite the dilapidated aspect of the capital city as the debris of the fire and the hurricane were slowly tidied away. More new buildings, more shops, more boarding houses and family residences went up to fill the straggling streets as the city rebuilt itself, though Pennsylvania Avenue was not to be paved for another fifteen years, when Jefferson's double rows of poplar trees were removed to widen the roadway, and elms were planted along each side in their place.

Styles were changing again, but Dolley kept to her elaborate feathered headdresses, and her personality was never overpowered by her clothes. "It is not her form; it is not her face; it is the woman altogether whom I should wish you to see," another Washington matron at that time wrote to her mother. "She wears a crimson cap that almost hides her forehead, but which becomes her extremely, and reminds one of a crown from its brilliant appearance contrasted with the white satin folds and her black curls; but her demeanor is so removed from the hauteur generally attendant on royalty that your fancy can carry the resemblance no further."

During the autumn the Madisons moved from the Octagon House to the corner residence in the brick row called Seven Buildings in Pennsylvania Avenue at 19th Street. The reason for this move has never been explained, but it is doubtful the Tayloe ghosts caused Dolley any uneasiness. Perhaps the Tayloes wanted their house back, or perhaps their violently Federalist convictions were a factor. The Seven Buildings house rose flush with the street on which its front windows faced, so that people passing by could look into the rooms on the ground floor. There is a tradition that children would gather outside to watch Dolley feed her pet macaw at the front window, which she did with an engaging little show for their amusement, encouraging the bird to squawk out words to make them laugh.

The famous receptions still took place, crowded into a smaller drawing room. There was a new sensation now, when the man who had saved New Orleans arrived in Washington—Andrew Jackson, Old Hickory to his devoted troops, was a spectacular figure in the social scene, wearing a uniform stiff with gold braid, his shock of gray hair and piercing eyes and tanned complexion marking him out for the rugged western Indian-fighter he had been since boyhood.

Although Jackson had been in Washington briefly before, as congressman for Tennessee, he was now a national novelty. He had married a divorced woman, whose jealous husband had contrived to turn the innocent affair into a scandal. He had fought several duels, and killed a man in at least one of them, and was notoriously quick to challenge. He had occupied the disputed city of Mobile and thrown out the Spanish and the British, and then, being without orders because of the confusion at the time of the British attack on Washington, he had gone on to take Pensacola, in November of 1814. Lastly he had inflicted the decisive defeat on the British at New Orleans in December, and made sure of the Mississippi. People who had scarcely heard of him till then crowded the many entertainments given in his honor, to make his acquaintance.

The presidential reception held for him in the modest Seven Buildings house was the greatest "squeeze," according to Mrs. Smith. The ladies all wore their best gowns and found his manner towards any and every female unexpectedly gentle, courteous, and full of a formal respect. His wife, who had endured a great deal for their love, was in failing health at their home in Nashville, and could not share his triumph.

In order to achieve the customary blaze of light which she considered essential to a gay evening, Dolley supplemented the lighting arrangements of the Seven Buildings drawing room by stationing liveried servants around the walls holding lighted candelabras. The refreshments were as always delicious and plentiful, the punch was strong, and the violins played constantly above the chatter.

Madison was suddenly popular, now that the war was won. The Federalist party, which had opposed him so bitterly, was dead. People spoke of "Mr. Madison's peace" now. Monroe, who had stood by his side so long, appeared to be the logical successor to the presidency, and his beautiful wife would be a gracious and experienced First Lady. By New Year's Day, 1816, the Madisons had begun to look forward to their retirement to Montpellier at the end of the second term with a gratified sense of duty well accomplished and perilous times safely survived with honor and distinction. But there was one casualty. Payne Todd.

Dolley's son by her first marriage was now a handsome, headstrong, overindulged young man of twenty-two, accustomed to being regarded by all as the president's son, for Madison had always considered him so. He had been sent to a boarding school at Alexandria at the age of eleven, and then to a Baltimore school, following the pattern of Madison's own boyhood which took him to Princeton at a tender age. But Madison was a born student, and at Baltimore Payne's exceptional good looks and precocity made him a social pet while he was still in his teens. He learned to hand the ladies in and out of their carriages and to the dinner table with grace, dance all the newest steps, and make himself agreeable to the flattered hostesses who were glad to add him to their eligible bachelor lists. It was believed at home that he was better off in Baltimore's civilized surroundings than in unfinished Washington, where so many crude amusements and temptations flourished to entice an idle young man to gambling, cockfighting, horse racing, tavern drinking, and the company of easy women of the lowest order.

Payne's connections made him conspicuous to the type of people who preyed on the young sons of rich and influential families, and he seemed to offer very little resistance, but went with the wind, willing to indulge in any amusement offered him. When Edward Coles's health failed and he went to Philadelphia to consult the doctors there, Payne was brought to Washington from Baltimore and given the opportunity to learn to make himself useful as Madison's secretary. He was not at all interested in employment he considered tedious, and Dolley did the work of copying and letter-writing which he should have accepted with gratitude. Unmoved by the industrious, responsible habits of his mother and stepfather, Payne drifted into the taverns and alleys as though in direct defiance of the two people who set him such a fine example.

When the peace commission sailed for Ghent in 1813 the president in desperation had arranged for Payne to accompany the son of one of its members, perhaps in some minor secretarial capacity. Dolley hoped that a change of surroundings and a wider horizon might check the boy's tendency to idleness and unfit companions. It was somewhat such an opportunity as John Quincy Adams had embraced when his father went abroad to represent America at the end of the Revolution. John Quincy had taken advantage of the chance to improve himself and returned with several languages at his command to take a professorship at Harvard. But Payne was reluctant even to go, and was determined not to profit from the adventure. European society made much of him, as the American president's "son," and he learned a little French and some new dance steps, and soon left the commission in order to jaunt around Europe with a young friend—during which time Dolley seldom heard from him and often had no idea where he was. When he needed more money he wrote to Richard Cutts for it, instead of to his mother, and Cutts had no choice but to honor his bills.

Payne had returned to Ghent by the time the news reached there of the British invasion of Washington, which was followed by the signing of the treaty. The illness of one of the American commissioners delayed their sailing after that, and Payne did not arrive in Washington till the autumn of 1815, about the time the Madisons moved into the Seven Buildings.

Dolley had not seen him for nearly two years, and found him much improved in looks and poise—which had also increased his conceit. He had spent a great deal of money, which Madison must now make good. Payne at once became very popular with the younger set in Washington, and there were many rumors of his attachment to this girl or that. Dolley hoped that he would marry, but the one serious affair which might have sobered him up ended by the young lady's refusing him, which cast him again upon the town.

As Dolley packed to leave the Seven Buildings house for the journey home to Montpellier, she nursed one last despairing hope—that having made the Grand Tour abroad and rejected nearly every career open to him, Payne would now settle down to the life of a country squire and heir to the Madison acres. It should have occurred to her that if only because of the life he had led so far, Montpellier to Payne could only represent the utmost boredom.

15

Piedmont Paradise

The Madisons attended the inauguration of their friend Monroe, which was the first to take place out of doors, on a mild day in March, 1817. As the Capitol Building had been so completely burnt out as to be still useless, a temporary "elevated portico" was hastily erected in front of the new brick building in which both Houses had been meeting separately since the fire. An enthusiastic crowd filled the streets below the platform and strained to hear the speeches which eulogized the outgoing president for bringing order out of the chaos which had reigned when he first took office. Monroe's address chiefly listed the national blessings of peace, security, a growing prosperity, and the triumph of the republican form of government which he had inherited from his predecessors.

The reception was held in the house in the Seven Buildings row which Dolley had been packing to vacate in time, although the Monroes preferred to return to their own house in I Street while the White House was being made ready to receive them. The Madisons remained long enough to bestow their blessing and good will on the new president, and for their homeward journey to Montpellier made use of a new form of transportation, as described by a friend who shared with them the first part of the journey:

"I accompanied him [Madison] in the steam-boat as far down the Potomac as Aquia Creek, where his carriage waited for him; and if ever a man rejoiced sincerely in being freed from the cares of public life it was him. During the voyage he was as a child; talked and joked with everybody on board, and reminded me of a schoolboy on a long vacation."

Like Washington and Jefferson before him, Madison was now free to retire to his beloved plantation world and become a full-time farmer. What he had once described as a "vortex of house-building" had resulted in a long, roomy mansion with a wing on each side of the original square built by his father, and a Doric portico which reflected Jefferson's classic taste. There were tall French windows, and a handsome fireplace in every room, and the drawing room mantelpiece had been sent from France years ago by Jefferson. Monroe when he became minister to France was commissioned to buy more furnishings for Montpellier in Paris, where the markets bulged with the abandoned treasures of the ruined French nobility and the emigrés who had fled from the guillotine. Madison's bed, with high posts and a canopy, had come from the dismantled Tuileries Palace.

The house had an airy effect of spaciousness and light, silk draperies at the long windows, gay carpets, delicate French chairs, fine paintings, classic busts—and on the upper floor a library so full of books that they eventually crowded Madison out to work in his sitting room, which adjoined the dining room with a door between, and which was furnished with a bed and writing desk. It was his habit when feeling below par to dine at a small table drawn up to the open doorway so that he could converse with his guests at the dinner table without leaving his room.

The members of his family, whose huge farms lay within a day's travel, included his brother William, his sisters Mrs. Macon and Mrs. Conway, and his niece Mrs. Willis. Dolley's sister Anna and her husband and the Cutts children were favorites of Madison's too, and Mary Cutts wrote of the relationship between Madison and her aunt as she recalled it from childhood:

"Mr. Madison dearly loved and was proud of his wife, the ornament of his house—she was his solace and comfort. No matter how agreeably employed, he was her first thought, and instinct seemed to tell her when she was wanted; if engaged in conversation she would quickly rise and say, 'I must go to Madison.' "

The "old wing" on the right of the entrance was inhabited exclusively by Madison's aged mother, who seldom joined the family circle, but took her meals separately in her own rooms, which were furnished with the heavy carved and polished mahogany and rich dark fabrics of her early married days. She was waited upon by her own servants, who had grown old in their devoted care of her. The Madisons visited her daily at 2 P.M., which was her hour for receiving, and would find her sitting upright on her sofa with her knitting and the books by Pope, Steele, Addison, and the Bible, which occupied her time, for her eyesight was still so good that she read without glasses.

Special guests were permitted to enter her apartments at this time of day, when she told them proudly of Dolley's care of her, often saying, "She is *my* mother now." Favored friends and relatives sometimes received socks and gloves knitted by "the old lady," as she was affectionately known to everyone, with no disrespect intended.

Madison had to sell some of his western lands to finance the improvements at Montpellier, but he still owned between three and four thousand acres. The house, according to Mrs. Smith who was a frequent visitor there, stood "on a height commanding an extensive view of the Blue Ridge, which by the constant variations in the appearance of the clouds and consequently the mountains form a very agreeable and varied aspect, sometimes appearing very distant, sometimes much separated and distinct, and often like rolling waves."

Tobacco was Montpellier's sustaining crop, along with grain to feed the livestock. There was an excellent vegetable garden, and a mill, and a community of well-treated slaves. The nearest town was Orange Courthouse five miles away, where the tavern served also as a schoolhouse. At the same time, it dispensed the raw whiskey provided by Madison for his harvest-hands, and which was not too rough for Payne's undiscriminating palate. An attempt by Madison to substitute beer for this potent beverage was a dismal failure.

Montpellier after the Madisons' retirement supplied the same hospitality that the White House had done while they lived in Washington. Wine, pineapples, and cakes were offered to unexpected visitors at any hour. Dinner was a ceremony in accordance with Madison's rather old-fashioned custom, when everyone changed into formal dress. Three or four kinds of meat were served, and as many kinds of bread; fresh vegetables, fresh fruit, pastries, and iced champagne; and after dinner, for the gentleman, the best "segars," till the room was blue with smoke. It had been caustically remarked by one of the more frugal diplomatic hostesses in Washington that Dolley's dinner table was "more like a harvest-home supper than the entertainment of a high official." To which Dolley replied that to her, "abundance was preferable to elegance; that circumstances formed customs, and customs formed taste; and as the profusion so laughed at by foreigners arose from the happy circumstance of the superabundance and prosperity of our country, she did not hesitate to sacrifice the delicacy of European taste for the less elegant, but more liberal, fashion of Virginia."

At the back of the house, beyond a long piazza, lay a vast green lawn where meals were often served in the summer. And the piazza, as at Mount Vernon, provided the master with a sheltered place to take his exercise in any weather. He was sixty-six when he retired, and he undertook the full management of the estate from then on, with no steward to assist him till just before his death. He hired a French gardener named Beazée, to design and supervise a place southeast of the house which was enclosed in a low brick wall and laid out in terraces of rose beds and box hedges for Dolley's special pleasure. Beazée and his wife had come to Virginia to escape the French Revolution, and Mme. Beazée was a voluble, good-hearted woman who occupied herself by teaching French to the young Negroes. She also concocted a tremendously ugly shade hat which the exquisite Dolley tactfully wore during her hours spent in the sun among her flowers. She shared her husband's busy retirement as completely and as readily as she had shared with him the stress and strain of the presidential years. "Imagine if you can," she wrote gaily to her young Cutts nieces in Washington, "a greater trial to the patience of us farmers than the destruction of a radiant patch of green peas by frost!" She collected seeds and cuttings for her flower garden from far and wide, and watched their daily growth with devoted interest.

The steady procession of guests through the house seemed only to add to her enjoyment of country life and certainly left no time for loneliness. Mrs. Smith wrote that when there were twenty-three guests at once Dolley assured her that they had "house-room in plenty." In July, 1820, Dolley was writing to Anna in Washington:

"Yesterday we had ninety persons to dine with us at one

table—fixed on the lawn, under a thick arbor. The dinner was profuse and handsome, and the company very orderly. Many of your old acquaintances were here, among them the two Barbours. [The Barbours were witty, amusing brothers of some consequence in Virginia. It was said that "Phil aims at a horsehair and splits it; James aims at a barn door and misses it." Philip was a judge, and James had been governor of Virginia until 1812, when he went into the United States Senate.]

"We had no ladies except mother Madison, Mrs. Macon, and Nelly Willis [Madison's sister and niece]. The day was cool and pleasant; half a dozen only stayed all night with us, and they are now about to depart. Colonel [President] Monroe's letter this morning announces the advent of the French Minister; we expect him this evening, or perhaps sooner, though he may not come until tomorrow. But I am less worried here with a hundred visitors than with twenty-five in Washington—this summer especially. I wish, dearest, you had just such a country home as this. I truly believe it is the happiest and most true life, and would be so good for you and the dear children. Always your devoted sister. . . ."

So, receiving his newspapers, letters, and visits from old and new friends and loyal supporters, Madison kept abreast of the times even in his chosen seclusion, and he always had his books for company in his long, wakeful nights. It is safe to say that he was happier in his retirement than either Washington or Jefferson was able to be, as the financial embarrassments which plagued both Mount Vernon and Monticello had not yet begun at Montpellier and Dolley's generous nature warmed his hearth and graced his dinner table. Barbecues in the woods, where animals were roasted whole, and the meal served at a long table under the forest trees, were attended by farmer neighbors from roundabout with their wives and children. There was always a punch bowl, and usually a fiddler, and the free talk ranged from politics to agriculture and back again, till the end of the day.

Dolley's letters to Anna were full of affection and small household news, and so were her letters to Payne when she knew where to find him, for he had drifted away again, back to the fleshpots of Philadelphia or Washington, and was seldom heard from except when he needed money. Dolley's letters to him were pitiful in their obstinate devotion to a neglectful son, their lack of reproach for his unloving behavior, their pleas for him to return home when he found it convenient, and their tactful acceptance of his "business embarrassments" which she refused to recognize as gambling debts.

Her hope that he would marry some nice girl and settle down led her to renew her association with Anthony Morris and his country-bred daughter Phoebe, who had made a visit to Dolley in the White House just before the war and charmed everyone with her naive delight in the fashionable scene. Now some ten years had passed and pretty Phoebe was fading into spinsterhood with the care of her aging father. Dolley even prevailed upon Payne to visit the Morris farm at Bolton in Pennsylvania, with some idea that Phoebe at her housekeeping duties might rouse in him some interest in domesticity. He apparently went just to please her, or to relieve himself of a tedious argument. He stayed two days, making himself agreeable enough, and then escaped to Philadelphia without committing himself to whatever hopes had been raised in Phoebe's heart by the undertaking. Thereafter his long, mysterious absences continued to cause uneasiness at Montpellier, and Dolley's affectionate, anxious letters flowed out to whatever address she thought might reach him:

"Yours, dearest, promising to write me again, came safely, and I was glad to hear that mine, with the inclosure, had reached you. You did not tell me whether you had been successful in your collections. If not, you will want supplies, and I am anxious that you should have them, and you know the little I have in my power is at your command, though but 'a drop in the bucket.' You will tell me when you intend to return, that I may have the pleasure of expecting you.

"Mr. Madison is better, though very ill a few days since, and I now hope he will soon be well enough for me to leave him for an expedition to the [Orange] Courthouse. It will be quite an event for me to go there, five miles from home! Our last tobacco was a failure; it sold at seven when seventeen was expected; so it goes with planters.

"Dolly and Mary wrote me yesterday that you were very popular in Washington and I should like to be with you to witness it—respect and love shown to my son would be the highest gratification the world could bestow on me. I think to enclose this to my brother to deliver in case of your having left, to keep it for your return when you are at home, as I shall enclose. . . ."

Money was enclosed, of course—whatever she could find for him.

A little later she wrote to him again:

"Everyone inquires after you; but my dear son, it seems to be the wonder of them all that you should stay away from us for so long a time! and now I am ashamed to tell, when asked, how long my only child has been absent from the home of his mother. Your father and I entreat you to come to us; to arrange your business with those concerned so that you may return to them when necessary, and let us see you here as soon as possible with your interest and convenience. Your father thinks as I do, that it would be best for your reputation and happiness, as well as ours, that you should consult your parents on subjects of deep account to you, and that you would find it so on returning to Philadelphia at the appointed time, which shall be whenever you wish it. I have said in my late letters as well as this, all that I thought sufficient to influence you. I must now put my trust in God alone.

"I enclose you $30 instead of the $20 you mentioned, and though I am sure it is insufficient for the journey, I am unable to add to the sum today. I recently paid Holloway $200 on your note, with interest for two years. I hope you will write me the moment you get this, that I may know certainly your determinations and make up my own.

"I can add no news that is likely to interest you, except about poor Judge Todd, who is very ill; and that Ellen Randolph is to be married to Mr. Coolidge. We should rejoice in any occurrence that would bring you speedily to our arms, who love you with inexpressible tenderness and constancy. Your own MOTHER."

Madison took a fatherly interest likewise in young Richard Cutts, who was a much more promising boy than Payne Todd had ever been, and both the Madisons were devoted to Anna's two daughters, Mary and Dolly. Several letters to them from their aunt have been preserved:

"I received by the last post a letter from your cousin Payne at New York," she was able to report at one time. "He writes in fine health and spirits, and says he will be detained only a few weeks longer in that city. I sincerely hope to see him soon, though it is impossible for him to prefer Virginia to the North.

"If I were in Washington with you I know I could not conform to the formal rules of visiting they now have, but would disgrace myself by rushing about among my friends at all hours. Here I find it most agreeable to stay at home, everything around me is so beautiful. Our garden promises grapes and figs in abundance, and I shall not enjoy these unless your mamma comes and brings you to help us with them; tell the boys they must come too. Adieu, and believe me always your tender mother and aunt. . . .

"P.S. We are very old-fashioned here. Can you send me a paper pattern of the present sleeve, and describe the width of dress and waist; also how turbans are pinned up, bonnets worn, as well as how to behave in the fashion!"

Happy as she was in her Piedmont paradise, Dolley's interest in clothes and society was not forfeit, and rumors of the somewhat starchy White House régime under Mrs. Monroe had piqued her curiosity.

16

A Labor of Love

News from Washington trickled down to Montpellier and was eagerly received and discussed at Dolley's fireside. By the autumn of 1818 the White House had been restored within and without for occupancy by the president, although the alterations and additions to the Capitol Building would make that reconstruction job take much longer.

Under Hoban's supervision the interior of the President's House was duplicated from his original plans as closely as possible, though on a somewhat grander scale. Even the famous oval rooms were restored, and remain a feature of the present building despite all subsequent repairs and additions. The furnishing was done by the Monroes on a $50,000 appropriation from Congress. Most of the furniture, as well as the china, and the chef, was brought over from France, and represented the excellent taste Eliza Monroe had acquired during her years abroad. Some of their own possessions, such as silver and table linens, even bearing their monogram, were also placed in use.

The new White House, in its gleaming coat of fresh paint, was first opened to the public for the New Year's Day reception in 1819. Monroe at fifty-nine was tall and raw-boned like Jefferson, but he was not a brilliant man, not an especially charming one, though he had Virginian good manners and a proper sense of the dignity of his office. There has always been a small, separate tribe of know-it-alls who seem to exist only for the satisfaction (to themselves) of criticizing the elected man in the White House, regardless of political party or personal values. These dubbed Madison's successor "James the Lesser" and "James the Second," with deliberate malice.

Mrs. Monroe was a beautiful woman who had figured regally at the Continental capitals and European courts during her husband's foreign ministries. She was well equipped, if she had chosen, to surpass Dolley Madison as the White House hostess, but she lacked Dolley's outgoing nature and warmth of heart, and she was one of those who had disapproved of Dolley's harvest-feast menus. She at once withdrew into the stiff formality she had observed abroad, and imposed a new etiquette on Washington society.

On the grounds that she had become a chronic invalid, she felt justified in designating certain restricted visiting hours when she would be available to callers, and she delegated the return calls to her married daughter Eliza Hay, as she felt herself unequal to that obligation. Mrs. George Hay was no diplomat, found her duties a bore, did not know how to make friends, and followed her own rather snobbish ideas on the ritual of "visiting." A feminine war of etiquette and precedence was soon raging, with bitter boudoir disputes over who should call on whom *first*, and if and when the call should be returned. Offended Washington ladies began to boycott Mrs. Monroe's fortnightly receptions, which were notoriously dull and where the refreshments were limited to wine, tea, coffee, and iced cakes. Even the husbands became embroiled by their wives in a social situation which threatened to become ridiculous. Dolley, who received rather one-sided reports lamenting her absence, was divided between dismay and laughter.

There was actually a story that, lacking the intervention of a tactful hostess like Dolley, insults were exchanged between the British and French ministers at a White House dinner party where neither Mrs. Monroe nor any other ladies were present. The two men left the table abruptly and crossed swords with each other in the hall, before Monroe could interfere. Arriving incredulously upon the spectacle of two men fighting a duel inside the White House, Monroe threw up their swords with another, ordered the duelists into separate rooms and kept them there while he sent for their carriages. He saw each of them into his own vehicle and waited till they drove away before he returned to the dinner table to finish the meal. Both ministers sent him an apology the next morning.

A German baron, having come to Washington with a letter of introduction from the American minister at Stockholm, attended one of Mrs. Monroe's receptions and left his impressions of Dolley's successor, who considered a nod from the receiving line sufficient welcome to a guest:

"Mrs. Monroe's Courts, or as they are called here, levees, are very interesting for one who in some degree can make a comparison with the Court etiquette of the Old World. From the entrance hall below one comes *à plein pied* into a large and attractive rotunda; a little to the left of the center of this room stood Mrs. Monroe. On arriving all go up to her and bow, and she answers the greeting with a little nod of the head. Mrs. Monroe was very elegantly dressed; her costume consisted of a white gown of Indian mull, embroidered with gold, her hair was braided with pearls and adorned with a lovely diadem of gold set with pearls, and ornaments of pearls adorned her throat, arms, and ears. She seemed to be between thirty and forty years old, medium sized, her face set off to advantage by her beautiful hair.

"At the Court was a large gathering of all classes and ranks of the community; and, as I judge, every free American that owns ground or carries on his business has the right to appear at the Courts of the President's wife. Foreign ministers, consuls, travellers, American officers and officials were quietly dressed, partly in uniforms, partly in plain clothes; but there were also others, badly and slouchily dressed, who seemed to want to display themselves in a costume less tidy and less suitable to the occasion. I noticed some farmers or other men in stained clothes, uncombed hair, unbrushed and muddy boots just as they had come from the street, whose figures contrasted sharply with the rest of the gathering. At one of the Courts I attended there was also a Chief of the Creek tribe, together with some of his Indians, dressed according to the custom of their people."

An American visitor about the same time noted that "Mr. Monroe still retains his plain and gentle manners, and is in every respect a very estimable man."

In time Mrs. Monroe was to live down her first chilliness and be on more cordial terms with most of the Washington hostesses. Her daughter Eliza Hay remained aloof, and when the arrangements for her younger sister Maria's wedding to their cousin Samuel Gouverneur were left to Mrs. Hay, so many names were omitted from the invitation list that much offense was taken. The ceremony took place in the Oval Room, and the reception in the great East Room, which had just been furnished and opened to the public. It was the first wedding in the renovated White House, which has seen so many since then.

The streets of Washington still were not paved in the 1820s, there was no drainage or sanitation, and the only water came from private wells. Epidemics of fever and "sore throat" were frequent and severe, as flies and mosquitoes swarmed, and snakes found their way into the drawing rooms. Cattle and sheep grazed within a stone's throw of the White House, and in the streets the vacant lots between new houses created the effect of missing teeth.

Monroe was re-elected with a large majority vote and was inaugurated for the second time in March, 1821, wearing a suit of black broadcloth in the "antiquated fashion" of knee-breeches and silk stockings, which was still assumed by conservatives for formal attire. It was a day of sleet and mud, which diminished the crowd gathered to see him pass along Pennsylvania Avenue in an "unostentatious carriage" drawn by four horses, with a single footman in livery. This time the ceremony took place in the chamber of the restored House of Representatives (now the Statuary Hall) which was crowded with the diplomatic corps and members of Congress. The Marine Band played "The President's March," making its first appearance as the official music of a government ceremony, as it has remained ever since. Everyone then adjourned to the White House for the reception, and the ball that year was held at Brown's Hotel on Pennsylvania Avenue at 6th Street. The president and his wife, who complained of fatigue, left before supper was served.

As Monroe's secretary of state, John Quincy Adams had been able finally to resolve the perpetual Florida question by a treaty which acquired the disputed territory from Spain forever, for the sum of five million dollars. Andrew Jackson was appointed governor of the Florida Territory. Jackson quarreled with everybody in sight during his tenure, and resigned within a year to return to his home at Nashville, convinced that Monroe had done nothing to support him in a difficult situation.

Adams shared with Monroe the labor and the credit for

establishing what has been known ever since as the "Monroe Doctrine." This was essentially a declaration that "the United States would consider dangerous to its peace and safety any attempt on the part of the European powers to extend their system to any point in the Western Hemisphere; and that the United States would not interfere with existing colonies of European powers in the New World, nor interfere in the internal affairs of European nations." At the time of its announcement in 1824 it received very little notice by the said powers. But having been modified and extended to meet later circumstances, it is still of major significance in international affairs.

By the time the election of 1824 came up, the Federalist party had quite disappeared, and only the Republicans, then a term still interchangeable with Democrats, remained, much divided among themselves on such questions as tariffs, banking, and slavery. The first Monroe administration had been one of peace regained, and a growing prosperity, and had become known as the Era of Good Feeling. This was bound to end. The 1824 campaign was a bitter contest of personal and sectional bias, with several very vocal candidates determined to win.

John Quincy Adams, secretary of state, represented the North against what had long ago been named by its enemies "the Virginia Dynasty." Against him stood John Calhoun, an Indian-fighter from the Carolina uplands turned congressman, and Senator Henry Clay from Kentucky. Andrew Jackson, of New Orleans and Florida fame, became the popular idol of the rough frontiersmen with whom he was closely identified as a resident of Tennessee. Monroe, the last of the old-school Virginia "gentlemen," retreated into cool neutrality among the personal conflicts which raged around him, even within his Cabinet. There was mudslinging in the press, and stump oratory full of invective and slander, overshadowing the larger political issues.

When the vote was counted in December, 1824, it was plain that Calhoun had won the vice-presidency, which since 1804 had been on a separate ballot, while there was no majority for any presidential candidate. Jackson led with 99 votes, far from enough, Adams was second with 54, Clay had only 37. For the second time, as in 1800, the election was thrown into the House of Representatives. The experienced, able, and cultivated Adams was the obvious choice over the turbulent wild man from Tennessee which was Jackson. Clay reluctantly threw his weight to the Massachusetts candidate, who had maintained a frigid dignity throughout the campaign, and had no knack of endearing himself to his associates or appealing to the general public, as Jackson had. Adams got the vote in the House, by a majority of 1, with Calhoun as vice-president, and Henry Clay as secretary of state. The Jacksonians now claimed to be the Democrats, and the party was finally split along that line, their opponents later to be known as Whigs, who may be said in a loose way to have evolved into what we now call Republicans.

Adams had been the American minister to Russia, Holland, and in 1815 to the Court of St. James. During his earlier travels abroad he had met and married a Maryland girl named Louisa Johnson, whose father was the American consul in London. Like Eliza Monroe, Mrs. Adams was in poor health and maintained the distant formality established at the White House since the Madisons had left it for Montpellier. After his years of training in the diplomatic service, Adams had a stiff and chilly manner and a poker face which never thawed into cordiality. When the ballots had been counted and Adams was announced as the winner, Monroe gave a reception at the White House which all Washington attended. Everyone there saw that the defeated candidate General Jackson was among the first to grasp the new president's hand and wish him well. Refreshments at the White House during Mrs. Adams's reign promised to be no more plentiful nor enlivening than those provided by Mrs. Monroe, and although the Marine Band played at the reception for Adams there was no dancing. Monroe in his turn followed Jefferson and Madison into retirement on a Virginia estate. He had built a house called Oak Hill in Loudoun County, and his old property near Monticello was sold to provide him with much needed funds.

At Monticello Jefferson was being eaten out of house and home by people who saved themselves a tavern bill by "paying their respects" to the former president. His daughter Martha Randolph resented these intrusions and refused, as she had done while he was in Washington, to aid him by performing the usual duties of a hostess for her father, on the grounds that she "had an aversion to company." Financial anxiety was now beginning to intrude at Montpellier also, with the price of tobacco still going down, and Payne's debts pouring in.

Many travellers went from one house to the other as a matter of course, and must have commented on the difference between their reception at Monticello, where an aging, harassed Jefferson was forced to cope with it alone, and at Montpellier, where Dolley's warm, extended hands were open to everyone who appeared.

The death of Thomas Jefferson at the age of eighty-three in 1826 brought to an end a friendship with Madison which had spanned fifty years. They had lately worked together to found the University of Virginia at Charlottesville. Jefferson sent to Montpellier by the doctor who had attended him his "gold-mounted walking-staff of animal horn," which Madison had seen in his hand on so many happy occasions. Madison was named to succeed Jefferson as rector of the University, which required his attendance at board meetings whenever he was well enough to travel. Dolley accompanied him on these trips, and they used Monticello as their headquarters during the visits until the house and its contents were sold at auction to settle Jefferson's impoverished estate.

There was a time when for some reason Dolley remained behind at Montpellier. One of the few letters she ever had occasion to write to her husband was sent after him to the university, and showed the passionate solicitude with which she followed his every move during their rare separations:

"My beloved—I trust in God that you are well again, as your letters assure me you are. How bitterly I regret not going with you! Yours of 'Friday midday' did not reach me till last evening. I felt so full of fear that you might relapse that I hastened to pack a few clothes and give orders for the carriage to be ready and the post waited for. This morning, happily the messenger has returned with your letter of yesterday, which revives my heart and leads me to hope you will be up at home on Wednesday night with your own affectionate nurse. If business should detain you longer — or you should feel unwell again, let me come for you. Mamma and all are well here. I enclose you one letter. The only one received by yesterday's post, with the two latest papers, to read on your journey back. I hope you received my last of Thursday morning containing letters and papers. My mind is so anxiously occupied about you that I cannot write. May angels guard thee, my dear best friend! D."

In the midst of the ordered confusion of his busy household, Madison worked doggedly at arranging and annotating his private papers and correspondence, intending them as his legacy to the congressional record. His recent labors had also included an extensive correspondence with Monroe during the latter's presidency, as Monroe had consulted his old friend on every presidential problem he encountered, and always received patient, valuable counsel. Madison's eyes tired easily now, and Dolley often absented herself from the drawing room to assist him, reading aloud from anything that interested him, and writing letters from his dictation.

Edward Coles, the invaluable bachelor secretary, had left their service before the end of Madison's second term, to go west to the Illinois Territory. He entered politics there, married, and became governor of Illinois. His pretty sister Sally was one of the many young women Dolley had hoped would interest Payne as a prospective wife, but Sally married Congressman Andrew Stevenson of Virginia, who was Speaker of the House, and maintained an affectionate correspondence with the Madisons after they retired to Montpellier. In 1826 Dolley wrote to Sally of her labors with Madison on his endless papers, and the confinement her attendance on his every need entailed:

"I have received by post just now, my ever dear cousin, your welcome letter, and cannot express my anxiety to embrace you once more; but a spell rests upon me, and withholds me from those I love in this world; not a mile can I go from home; and in no way can I account for it, but that my husband is fixed here, and hates to have me leave him. This is the third winter in which he has been engaged in the arrangement of his papers, and the business seems to accumulate as he proceeds, so that it might outlast my patience; and yet I cannot press him to forsake a duty so important, or find it in my heart to leave him during its fulfillment. We very often speak of you and the many causes of our admiration for you, concluding by reassuring each other that if we could leave home this winter it would be to visit you and Mr. Stevenson. Allow us, then, my dear, to retain the privilege you so kindly give us, of our rooms, where you shall some day see us.

"I receive letters every week from my sister Anna; she is in a round of pleasant society, and though devoted as ever to her children, takes time to enjoy a good dance.

Affectionately...."

So for the second time Dolley can be thanked for the preservation of Madison's private records. In 1814 she had sacrificed her personal belongings to make room for the boxes containing the president's papers, which saved them from the fire. Now she sacrificed her time and strength and contacts with family and friends to devote herself to Madison's arduous self-imposed task of editing and arranging his notes and correspondence from the days of the Constitutional Convention onwards. Eventually she too began to have some trouble with her eyes as a result of sharing the labor of her ailing husband, and before long an illness of Anna's was causing her great concern.

17

Three Deaths

John Quincy Adams held the presidency for only one term, and almost inevitably in 1828 he was swept out of office by the stormy petrel from Tennessee, Andrew Jackson—the seventh man to be elected in forty years, and the first frontier-born president.

In the same year the beloved "old lady," Madison's mother, died at Montpellier at the age of ninety-seven, and was buried in the cemetery at the foot of the flower garden.

In December, 1831, Dolley was writing to her niece Mary:

"I hope you will soon be going to parties, and give us a detailed account of what is going forward amongst the various characters in Washington. I have been so long confined by the side of my dear sick husband, never seeing or hearing outside of his room, that I make a dull correspondent.

"Your uncle is better now than he was three days ago, and I trust will continue to mend, but his poor hands are still sore and so swollen as to be almost useless, and so I lend him mine. The music-box is playing beside me, and seems well adapted to solitude, as I look out at our mountains, white with snow, and the winter's wind sounding loud and cold.

"I hope you will take more than usual care of yourself this weather, and wish I could cover you with furs; but ah! if I dare indulge in wishes—

"Good-night, my love. Your fond aunt. . . ."

Less than a year after this letter was written Anna Cutts, the beloved "sister-child" of Dolley's youth, died suddenly at her home in Washington. Dolley's famous natural buoyancy was for a while destroyed by shock and grief, but the necessity to uphold her husband's failing strength and to manage her large household on steadily diminishing funds required her to rally again to her daily duties. She found comfort in letters to and from Anna's daughters, in her books, and—lacking our modern diversions of radio and television—in her music boxes.

In 1835 she was writing to Mary Cutts during one of Payne's rare visits at home with a companion:

"Payne met a friend of yours yesterday at Orange Courthouse and brought him home to dinner, with his two cousins. We are much pleased with his society, as well as the account he gave of you and Dolly. He told me of your pleasant party and how much he admired you both, but not half as much about you as I want to know; indeed, how could he, when my love for you makes me wish to trace your every word and deed throughout the years. He gave me your letter, and told us about all the great personages now with you; but what was my grief to receive only one music-box! the box I prized—the one you and Dolly gave me—was missing! I will hope, however, that it was left with you, and I shall still hear it in these deep shades. Have you any amusing books, no matter how old, to lend me?

"Your inquiries after your uncle, and how we pass our time, can be more accurately answered. My days are devoted to nursing and comforting my sick patient, who walks only from the bed in which he breakfasts to another, in the little room in which you left him; he is a little better, but not well enough to get into a carriage and drive to the Springs, which I fondly hoped he might do. I expect Mrs. Randolph, Septimia, and two Misses Jefferson Randolph tomorrow, to pass a few days. My love to Richard, and accept my apology for this scrawl. Your own and always. . . ."

Madison's body was weak and suffering, but his mind remained alert and his memory never failed, though he was forced to rely more and more on Dolley's helping hands as he labored over his papers. He had never known a day of really robust health and vigor in his life, though he had ridden his beloved horses until restricted to carriage drives behind a shining, well-groomed team. He was finally too crippled by rheumatism to enjoy even the shortest outing. From his room next to the dining room, wearing a woolen dressing gown and cap, he could hear and join in the conversation while eating his own meal at the little table set in the open doorway.

Guests continued to come and go, from Lafayette in 1824 to Miss Harriet Martineau ten years later, when Madison was eighty-three. Miss Martineau, an intelligent, educated, travelled woman far ahead of her time, was accompanied by Miss Jeffries, a "sprightly" little middle-aged companion who assisted her with her packing and note-taking, for she was going to write a book about her experiences in America, and was so handicapped by deafness that she had to use an ear trumpet. The English "bluestocking" caught Madison's interest at once and was privileged to be much in his company during her stay of several days at Montpellier.

"The active old man, who declared himself to be crippled with rheumatism, had breakfasted, risen, and was dressed before we sat down to breakfast," Miss Martineau wrote. "He talked a good deal about the American presidents and some living politicians for two hours, when his letters and newspapers were brought in.

"He gayly threw them aside, saying he could read the newspapers every day and must make the most of his time with us, if we must go away as soon as we talked of. He asked me, smiling, if I thought it too vast an anti-republican privilege for the ex-presidents to have their letters and newspapers free, considering this was the only earthly benefit they carried away from their office."

On the whole, Miss Martineau was not enthusiastic about America, but she was impressed with the Madisons, and after Madison's death she wrote of Dolley: "For a term of eight years she administered the hospitalities of the White House with such discretion, impartiality, and kindliness, that it is believed she gratified everyone and offended nobody. She is a strong-minded woman, fully capable of entering into her husband's occupations and cares; and there is little doubt that he owed much to her intellectual companionship, as well as to her ability in sustaining the outward dignity of his office.

"When I was her guest she was in excellent health and lively spirits; and I trust that though she has since lost the great object of her life she may yet find interests enough to occupy and cheer many years of an honored old age."

Soon after Miss Martineau left Montpellier, Dolley felt at last compelled to stem the tide of visitors and wrote to an old friend who had proposed herself for a stay in the usual way: "I never leave my husband more than a few minutes at a time, and have not left the inclosure round my house for eight months, on account of his continued indisposition, of which friends at a distance have received too favorable reports. Our physicians have advised the Warm Springs, and we hoped to have taken him there; but as he could not travel unless conveyed in his bed, we dare not think of it at present. I can only express the hope, my dearest friend, that my husband will be well enough for us to have the gratification of seeing you here before the winter throws its barriers between us. Nothing would give us more pleasure than to welcome you and your daughter."

It must be remembered that in her care of her husband Dolley always had the support of Madison's colored body servant, Jennings, whose lifelong service to his beloved master became a legend. With someone's assistance Jennings was later able to record his own reminiscences of Madison's last years. "I was always with Mr. Madison till he died," Jennings wrote, "and I shaved him every other day for sixteen years. For six months before his death he was unable to walk, and spent most of his time reclined on a couch. But his mind was bright and with his visitors he talked with as much animation and strength of voice as I ever heard him in his best days." A further anecdote tells that Madison often asked his callers to draw their chairs close to his sofa, remarking with his twinkling smile, "I always talk better when I *lie*."

Charles Ingersoll, the congressman-author who had been selected to write Madison's life, noted in 1835 that Dolley "looks just as she did twenty years ago, and dresses in the same manner, with her turban and cravat; rises early and is very active, but seldom leaves the house, as her devotion to Madison is incessant, and he needs all of her constant attention."

Ingersoll was also the first visitor to comment on signs of decay and lack of repairs at Montpellier, evidence of growing financial distress and a slackening of its master's supervision.

Madison's death came "as quietly as the snuff of a candle goes out," according to Jennings, who had brought him a breakfast he could not eat, as his head fell back with a little sigh. It was late in June, 1836, and the Piedmont was in the full glory of summer. A hundred slaves stood weeping around the grave in the little brick-walled burying ground where his aged mother had been laid only a few years before.

The house was full of guests again, for Dolley's brother John had come from his home in Kentucky, accompanied by his daughter Anna. Mary Cutts was there, and Martha Randolph arrived with three of her daughters on a visit of condolence. Even Payne Todd conferred his presence on the grieving household for a few days. But Dolley had given up hope on Payne. She asked for her niece Anna to remain with her as "family" in place of the son on whom she could never rely for companionship or affection. John Payne returned to Kentucky without his daughter, and Anna, namesake of the "sisterchild," was to remain with her aunt for the rest of Dolley's life. Without her, Dolley would have faced an intolerable loneliness.

She bore up bravely through the many duties required by Madison's funeral and legal affairs. He had named her as his literary executrix, charged with the final arrangement of his papers left uncompleted at his death, and she took this task very seriously. A paper exists in her handwriting, apparently copied for him or taken down at his dictation, to be read after his death. It was headed "Advice to My Country," and ended with the words:

"The advice nearest my heart and deepest in my convictions is, That the Union of the States be cherished and perpetuated. Let the open enemy to it be regarded as a Pandora with her box opened, and the disguised one as the serpent creeping with his deadly wiles into paradise."

To the end he dreaded and anticipated the disunion leading to secession which he had more than once seen narrowly averted, and which was to come to another crisis within twenty-five years.

18

"A Young Lady
of Four Score Years"

Life went on almost as usual at Montpellier for a while after
its master's death. He had lately engaged an overseer who was
able to maintain the daily routine of the place as Madison had
desired. Dolley was occupied with replying to the many messages of condolence which poured in from everyone from
President Jackson down. Her eyes were giving trouble again
after months of overwork and days of unaccustomed weeping,
and young Anna took pride in learning to act as her aunt's secretary. Three clerks were brought in to finish copying the
manuscripts Dolley was working on when Madison died.

In her reply to the president Dolley wrote, at the end of her
letter: "The best return I can make for the sympathy of my
country is to fulfill the sacred trust his confidence reposed in
me, that of placing before it and the world what his pen prepared for their use, a legacy the importance of which is deeply
impressed on my mind."

Along with giving her the responsibility of preparing his
papers for their publication and inclusion in the Congressional

Library, where Jefferson's dearest treasures already resided, Madison had made Dolley the beneficiary of whatever monetary value would be placed on them. His own estimate of their worth was in the neighborhood of $100,000. The signers of the Constitution had agreed in 1787 that their deliberations should be kept secret for fifty years. That time was now almost elapsed.

Madison's private notes jotted down during the debates behind closed doors in Philadelphia were the only first-hand record of the proceedings, and he knew they were of supreme importance to history. He had edited and annotated them conscientiously, in spite of his growing disabilities and pain, and was occupied with his later notes and correspondence during his presidency when he died. It was left for Dolley to see this monumental work into print and the safekeeping of Congress. She wrote to Henry Clay in the Senate about "this charge, dear and sacred," which had sustained her in her recent loss, "and formed an oasis in the desert it created in my feelings."

In December, 1836, President Jackson recommended to Congress the immediate purchase of the Madison papers. In April Dolley's trunks containing the first installment, mainly those devoted to the Convention of 1787, were delivered to the secretary of state. As with Jefferson's library, Congress was niggardly. It voted $30,000 in payment to Madison's widow, plus the ownership of the stereotypes after printing. She had expected at least $50,000.

Disappointment, fatigue, and grief overtook her in the spring of 1837, and she allowed herself the luxury of a total collapse. Her devoted friend Anthony Morris came to Montpellier in his anxiety and persuaded her to take her doctors' advice and go to White Sulphur Springs for the "cure," which had benefited so many of her friends in the neighborhood. She found it "a new world to me who have never left Montpellier for nearly six years, even for a day," she wrote Morris after her return home in September.

She had spent two weeks at the Springs, "drinking moderately at the waters, and bathing my poor eyes a dozen times a day. The effect was excellent. My health was strengthened to its former standing, and my eyes grew white again; but in my drive home of six days in the dust they took a fancy to relapse a little. Still, I cannot refrain from expressing with my own pen (forbidden by you) my grateful sense of your kind friendship on every occasion. I met with many relatives and friends on my 'grand tour,' and had every reason to be gratified, but for my own sad, impatient spirit, which continually dwelt on my duties at home, still unfinished. In truth, my five weeks absence from Montpellier made me feel as if I had deserted my duties, and therefore was not entitled to the kindness everywhere shown me. And so I am at home at work again."

As soon as the clerks who had been hired to complete the transcripts had taken their departure, Dolley faced the oncoming mountain winter and a hard choice of where to establish herself for even the immediate future. Madison's books were being sent to the new university at Charlottesville, which would further empty the house of many dear associations of the spirit. The estate itself, though left solely to her, was encumbered with loans he had taken out in recent years just to keep things going as usual, and with legacies to his numerous family connections, who were jealous of Payne Todd's irresponsible position as Madison's adopted son. There remained for Dolley's consideration a house in Washington in the President's Square (which had been renamed Lafayette Square in 1824), a tree-shaded park north of the White House. Once an apple orchard on a farmstead, the square has since been landscaped and during the last hundred years its fine old houses have been preserved and occupied by private clubs and government departments.

The house at the corner of H Street and Madison Place on the square had been built by Richard Cutts in 1818, with money borrowed from his brother-in-law after the Madisons had left Washington. Cutts soon found he had overspent himself on the venture, and within ten years Madison assumed possession of the house to prevent its sale. The Cutts family continued to live there till after Anna's death.

Although she had never seen the house, for Dolley it had family associations with Anna and her daughters. In the autumn of 1837 she decided to make her winter home there, with her brother's daughter as a companion. She was compelled to use some of the money she had received from the sale of Madison's papers to put the house in repair and move into it some personal treasures and furniture from Montpellier.

It was a simple dwelling of buff-colored stucco, two stories with dormer windows, an attic, and a small garden in the rear. Its front door opened on the square, and faced the new North Portico of the White House, which was now occupied by Andrew Jackson's successor, Martin Van Buren. The president Dolley found in possession was a self-made New Yorker, who had risen through the secretary of state and vice-president route, as one of Jackson's followers.

Dolley returned to Washington as a widow of sixty-nine, attended by an excited girlish niece and the elderly colored maid Sukey, who had shared the flight from the British in 1814. Nearly twenty years had passed since she and Madison had seen Monroe installed in the White House and then taken the new steamboat down to Aquia before entering the carriage which waited there to take them home to Montpellier. Since then her life had been busy, demanding, and not in the least humdrum. She probably felt very little changed in herself, for she was in good health again, without infirmities. But Washington had changed, her circumstances had changed radically, and fashions too had changed.

The carefully preserved wardrobe of the elegant Dolley Madison was out of style. This was the year that the young Victoria was crowned queen of England. The clinging, classic outline of women's clothes as worn by the Empress Josephine had given way to elaborate bulk, padding, and tightly laced stays to constrict the waist. Sleeves were enormous at the shoulder, tight at the wrist. Skirts had widened and shortened to the ankle, with decorated hems. The narrow bodices were boned and often covered by the graceful sloping "pelerine," a wide flat collar with rounded ends which extended beyond the shoulder and spread over the ballooned sleeves. Hats were now bonnets, heavy with plumes and ribbons. The dress turban was still worn by matrons, and little lace caps with ribbons and strings were popular for indoor wear. Hair was parted smoothly in the middle, with curls covering the ears. It was "the thing" to appear languid and helpless, and "fainting" had become an art.

It can be seen that hearty, competent, highly-colored Dolley, who had not hesitated to brighten her naturally delicate complexion with rouge, found herself very much behind the times, but she was too impoverished to order new dresses from Paris and Philadelphia as she had used to do. Characteristically, she remained exactly as she had always been, without attempting to make herself over from the way she had appeared as the president's wife. People who rushed to welcome her back to town found her a reincarnation of the great days before the War of 1812, and could see at a glance that she had not inherited any great wealth. They respected her simple acceptance of her situation, which she never spoke of, and for which she made no apology.

Having brought her household goods from Montpellier, she was surrounded by her own good taste, living in her own era still, as the elder Mrs. Madison had done in the old wing at Montpellier while her son's wife filled their rooms with the contemporary French furniture chosen for them by Monroe and Latrobe.

One of Dolley's first callers in Lafayette Square was ex-President John Quincy Adams, who was living in Washington as representative for Massachusetts, and at the age of seventy had become a fixture in Washington society. Adams had been chosen to announce to Congress the sad news of Madison's death, and had spoken a generous and moving tribute to "the Father of the Constitution." In his private diary on October 24, 1837, he wrote:

"This morning I visited Mrs. Madison, who has come to take up her residence in this city. I had not seen her since March, 1809. The depredations of time are not so perceptible in her appearance as might be expected. She is a woman of placid appearance, equable temperament, and less susceptible to lacerations of the scourges of the world than most others. The term of her husband's presidency was tempestuous, but he weathered the storm by that equanimity which carried him also through an eventful period and a boisterous age. The two closing years of his presidency terminated his political life with honor and tranquillity. The succeeding twenty years she has passed in retirement—so long as he lived, with him, and now upwards of a year since his decease. She intended to have removed to this place last autumn, but was prevented by an inflammatory disease in her eyes, from which she has almost wholly recovered. There is no trace of it in her appearance now."

This is an interesting passage particularly because the entries in John Q.'s diary were seldom anything but embittered and highly critical of society as he found it. His failure to win a second term rankled, and his personal feud with the rough-hewn soldier-president Jackson was carried over to Van Buren as Jackson's friend and successor. He was famous for his ferocious congressional debates. His long knowledge of government affairs, his acquaintance with leaders dead and gone, his uncompromising convictions, and his caustic vocabulary made him a tough opponent in the Congress. He was not loved, but he was respected and feared. To Dolley he was simply another old friend, one who had supported the Louisiana Purchase and the unpopular embargo.

The little house at the corner of Lafayette Square was open to anyone who chose to renew acquaintance with her, though the list of those whose faces she would never see again was long. Worst of all, her sister Anna was gone, before they could have the opportunity of happy reunion under this very roof. For a while Dolley's old-fashioned hospitality flowed as freely as ever. Her old friends, who had never approved of Jackson's free and easy ways and hairy frontier cronies, welcomed her warmly and basked again in the serene social atmosphere of the great days of "the Virginia Dynasty."

Her former major domo, Sioussat, had become a prosperous American citizen as he desired, had married, and held a job with the bank. He returned to her with the offer of whatever service she might require, and he kept an experienced eye on her household and finances in more ways than she was aware of. Madison's stately and picturesque body servant, Jennings, had caught the envious eye of Daniel Webster during a visit Webster had made to Montpellier in 1824. Webster was then a promising congressman from Massachusetts, already known for his oratory, and in the showy political debates of the early 1830s his reputation had grown. His name had been mentioned for the presidency before Van Buren won in 1836 over poorly organized opposition.

Webster became one of Dolley's staunchest friends during her years in Lafayette Square. After he became secretary of state in 1841 he was also her neighbor, living in the Swann house a few doors away on Connecticut Avenue—a site now covered by the Chamber of Commerce Building. Webster entertained in great style, and his wife's friends were all anxious to meet the famous Dolley Madison. Dolley and young Anna were often invited to dine with the Websters and did much to keep alive the memories of the great days before Jackson's rowdy Democrats came crashing on to the Washington scene. After Madison's death Jennings became a member of Webster's household, and was working out his freedom at the rate of eight dollars a month with keep. When it became apparent as time went on that Dolley was forced to practice many humiliating little economies, it was a simple matter for Jennings to smuggle extra provisions into her pantry from Webster's well-stocked larder, with his master's full approval.

By an odd coincidence in 1837 there was another widower president in the White House, which was without a hostess until Van Buren's eldest son Abraham married the beautiful Angelica Singleton of Charleston in November, 1838. Young Mrs. Van Buren made her first appearance at the New Year's Day reception the following January. By tradition it was Dolley who filled that place by proxy, for Miss Singleton was the niece of Andrew Stevenson, who had married Dolley's cousin Sally Coles, and it was supposedly at Dolley's house in Lafayette Square that the president's son and the South Carolina beauty first met.

The interior of the renovated White House would have been of great interest to Dolley when she returned there as Van Buren's honored guest. Jackson, for all his backcountry ways, had had the good sense to take the sophisticated advice of his friend Van Buren from New York, when he undertook to furnish more of the rooms and add to what the Monroes had left there when they retired to Oak Hill. Jackson ordered his glass and silver and china from Europe, where Van Buren had traveled, and it was during Jackson's administration that the North Portico was completed, so that the main entrance faced Pennsylvania Avenue as had been the original plan, and as it still is. The South Portico already faced on the garden looking towards the swampy banks of the little creek called Tiber, where Constitution Avenue now runs above the underground course of the stream.

On New Year's Day, 1838, the White House visitors after paying their respects to the president at the usual reception, felt a lack, and flowed quite naturally across the square to enter Dolley's door, where they were cordially received, fed, and ushered smoothly out at the rear with experienced ease. After the July 4 reception at the White House the same thing happened. And so it remained throughout her life, an unofficial, spontaneous, personal tribute to her past and current popularity.

The diarist Philip Hone, who circulated in Washington society, remarked of Dolley: "She is a young lady of four score years, who goes out to parties, and receives company like the 'Queen' of this New World." It was hard for the younger generation to realize that she was still short of eighty. With her niece "Annie," who had proved a most congenial companion, at her side, Dolley resumed her Washington routine as before, almost as though those twenty years of exile at Montpellier had never happened. She paid the customary calls, accepted invitations to dinner in the best society, and gave little receptions at her house which, as her finances dwindled, were still not stinted in their hospitality.

The Cutts family of nieces and nephews lived nearby in 14th Street. Their father's fortunes had declined rapidly after Jackson came in with his noisy Democrats and in their favor had ousted the men whom the Virginia presidents had left in the security of small government posts. The financial depression of 1837 completed their ruin.

Young Richard Cutts had fallen in love with Martha Jefferson Hackley and Dolley encouraged the match, urging Richard to "secure for your life and even after, the lonely one who has promised you her hand—who I am persuaded is a prize to any man." The young people married in the face of many doubts and obstacles, and Dolley gave them a wedding reception no one ever forgot. The marriage of a Jefferson connection with a Madison nephew was an occasion which brought all Washington society to the little house on the square to offer their congratulations and wish the young couple happiness. Dolley had earned the everlasting devotion of Richard and Martha Cutts, who would help to fill the void left by her own tragic son, Payne Todd.

19

Pride and Poverty

Perhaps in the effort to separate Payne from the low companions he always found in Washington or Philadelphia, and bring him to some belated sense of responsibility—at the age of forty-three—Dolley had left him at Montpellier to manage the estate with the aid of an overseer named Dixon who had been trained by Madison. In the unwanted solitude—which his obstinate refusal to marry had imposed upon him—Payne went downhill very fast. He drank too much, alone, and in search of some one to gamble with he disappeared for days, to the despair of Dixon, who was not entrusted with the keys Payne always took with him. Dixon in consequence wrote to Dolley that he could not get at the stores to give the harvesthands the bacon and whiskey they would not work without. Even the slaves sent her unhappy bulletins that they were all well, and "Master J. P. Todd is well but aint at home." He had become overly suspicious of everyone, and his letters to his mother were full of pompous advice and warnings against imaginary "Trojan horses" among her Washington acquaintances. In his loneliness he kept a rambling, rather incoherent diary where his exaggerated self-importance warred with his well-justified self-doubt.

Madison's death seemed to have removed Payne's last prop and anchor. His mother's departure to Washington had thrown him back on himself, confronted with daily obligations he had no idea how to meet. For the first time in his wasted life he was on his own, without Madison's support and guidance and his mother's pampering solicitude. He simply went to pieces.

The plantation economy on which estates like Montpellier, Monticello, and Mount Vernon had always depended was a false one, requiring the constant supervision of an experienced and conscientious master, or it lost money, deteriorated, and became incapable of supporting itself. Payne's incompetence and neglect reduced Dolley's income, brought on new debts, and bred a general sense of insecurity and doom. Madison had foreseen the end of his Piedmont empire, which could only have been postponed for perhaps another generation by careful management. In Payne's hands the situation rapidly became hopeless.

Dolley had always intended to return to Montpellier for the summers, as she had done during Madison's lifetime. In June, 1839, when she arrived there she decided to remain and learn to be a "farmeress," in the hope of salvaging something from the wreck Payne had made of things. But Madison had not taught her how he ran the estate, as he had taught her his literary labors, and she had no natural head for business. For the last time Montpellier warmed and bloomed in her presence, guests came and went, and her sister Lucy, widowed again by the death of Judge Todd, joined her and Annie to bring laughter and love into the cold, lonely rooms. Lucy even tried to match-make again for Payne, without success.

Dolley remained at Montpellier for more than two years, while Sioussat kept watch over the house in Lafayette Square and a lively correspondence went on between them. She was able to add a mite to her income by renting the house under his supervision to various homeless congressmen, who found a comfortable lodging there by bringing in their own servants.

While she was away at Montpellier the election of 1840 took place, bringing in the aging General Harrison, hero of the battle of Tippecanoe. Harrison was elected to represent the Young Republicans headed by Henry Clay against the remnants of the Jackson regime. The vice-president was chosen solely to hold the Southern vote—John Tyler, one-time governor of Virginia, of the Old Republican school as founded by Jefferson, and a known dissenter to the very things Harrison was supposed to stand for. No one anticipated that Harrison would die of pneumonia a month after his inauguration, and leave Tyler in possession of the power the Whigs had hoped to wield through the man they had put in office. Tyler was of course the first vice-president to succeed to office by the death of his predecessor.

When Dolley returned to Washington in the autumn of 1841 John Tyler was in the White House and all Washington was at sixes and sevens. This time the president's wife was again a confirmed invalid, and his son Robert's young wife found her official duties frightening. She did not hesitate to consult Mrs. Madison, who came to her assistance with great good will, so that it was soon remarked in the press that the White House entertainments had a charm which had never been felt since the days when the Madisons "gave tone and polish to American society." Dolley seemed to her friends vigorous and hopeful, she accepted most of the invitations which rained in on her, enjoyed going out to receptions and dinner parties, and was in great demand everywhere. Young Mrs.

Tyler gave her a prominent place on official occasions, and always reserved a seat in the president's carriage for her. It is interesting that none of her successors in the White House ever showed any jealousy of Dolley's continued prestige and influence, but had only admiration for her and confidence in her private counsel.

There was still a sizable amount of Madison's presidential papers in her possession, and Dolley was anxious to realize on them for her day-to-day expenses. She had been advised that publication by a commercial firm would be more profitable than another sale to Congress, and she had already approached Harper's in New York with the congressional stereotypes and the later material still in her possession. But when she went to New York in the spring of 1842, travelling behind the new steam engine, it was on another and more confidential matter.

She had decided to take out a mortgage on the Lafayette Square house, which was in her name, for her immediate expenses. She was confident that the publication of her husband's papers would enable her to repay it before it fell due, but the returns might be slow, and her need was pressing. Her pride would not allow her to turn to anyone in Washington for a loan, but she had one friend in New York who had come to the aid of the government in the dark days of 1812, and had sent gifts of wine and tea to the Madisons at that time. His name was John Jacob Astor.

It was an entirely businesslike arrangement, requiring the history of the title and all legal guarantees, and resulted in a mortgage of $3000 for seven years at 6 per cent. By the time she reached Montpellier again in the summer of 1842 she was exhausted and depressed. There is some evidence that Payne Todd undertook with his usual self-confidence to negotiate with Harper's himself on her behalf, and went to New York for that purpose. He of course fell in with all the wrong people and succeeded in causing only confusion and delay. In desperation Dolley turned back to Congress with the offer of the remaining volumes of Madison's literary bequest. A motion was made in the Senate for their purchase as before, but as often happens the House did not follow through and the thing got shelved.

Meanwhile she sold off some land at Montpellier, and finally consented to rent the house itself for a period of three years, and returned to her mortgaged home in Washington. Before long she sold Montpellier outright to Henry Moncure of Richmond, to save it from seizure by the sheriff for debt. Her last obstinate dream of Montpellier's passing to her son as his heritage was gone. Moreover, his unsavory reputation had become more widely known as a result of another of his wild business ventures, and President Tyler had curtly refused Dolley's request to name him to a diplomatic post abroad.

In the spring of 1845 there was a new president in the White House—James K. Polk, the "dark horse" from Tennessee, whose wife was the first since Mrs. John Quincy Adams who was adequate to her position. She and Dolley had been friends since 1837 when Polk was the Democratic congressman from Tennessee. Sara Polk was a dark-haired, handsome, cultivated woman, childless, who like Dolley was accustomed to act as her husband's secretary. She was well-read, a good conversationalist, with "an excellent taste in dress." There was one drawback. Her strict Presbyterian background was more unyielding than Dolley's Quakerism had been. Dancing, cards, and alcoholic refreshment were all banned at the White House under her rule. But the disappointed diplomats and congressmen knew where to find the traditional amenities, and trooped happily across the square after the arid presidential entertainments. Dolley provided, with her usual good nature and cordiality, and there is no evidence that any difficulties arose between the two ladies as a consequence of her hospitality.

Without Montpellier as a summer home, Dolley and Annie were forced to spend the humid summer days in deserted Washington, and Annie contracted the terrible Potomac malaria and was very ill for five months. This meant doctors' bills and medical bills, and for once the interest on Dolley's mortgage went unpaid, and word of her worsening circumstances leaked out. Daniel Webster in the goodness of his heart evolved an idea of raising an annuity by subscription for her benefit, which she promptly rejected as beneath the dignity of Madison's widow. Webster's concern penetrated to Congress, which had still not acted on the purchase of Madison's remaining papers. At Christmas time, 1847, a committee waited on Dolley to offer a trust fund of $25,000 which would provide her with an annual income on which she and Annie could survive.

When the committee learned of the mortgage—due the following year—and the little bank loans and the pawned silver and other pathetic expedients she had already been put to, they hastily released the first $5000 to set her straight again. They were sufficiently aware of Payne's character not to turn over the entire sum to his indulgent mother, for her own protection. The bill was passed by Congress in time for Dolley's eightieth birthday on the twentieth of the following May, and congratulations poured in from her friends and well-wishers. To Dolley the safe bestowal of her husband's papers had become more important than the sum which could be wrung from the recipients for her future welfare.

The promise of relief from financial worry brought a quick rebound in her spirits. In February 1849, she attended a reception in the East Room of the White House, given by President

Polk as his farewell after the election of Zachary Taylor the previous autumn. She wore a new white satin gown—the trust fund—and a white satin turban with fringe, for it was a State occasion. There was rouge on her cheeks and the old illuminating smile turned up the corners of her mouth. In Polk's diary he wrote: "It was what could be called in the society of Washington a very fashionable levee. Foreign Ministers, their families and suites, Judges, members of both Houses of Congress, and many citizens and strangers were of the company present. I stood and shook hands with them for over three hours. Towards the close of the evening I passed through the crowded rooms with the venerable Mrs. Madison on my arm."

She was a great lady, a greatly beloved lady, and Polk conducted her on a sort of promenade so that everyone might see her and touch her hand. It seemed natural to Dolley, who had always circulated among her guests when the receptions had been held in the Oval Room. Mrs. Polk as naturally ceded to her her old place as First Lady. It was an evening long remembered by all who were present.

20

Last Will
and Testament

When the news of the trust fund reached Payne Todd he
stormed into Washington threatening vengeance against those
who had tied up his mother's money beyond his reach, and
threatening to sue the trustees, who were all her old friends.
His debts at that time had mounted to something like $10,000,
and he was desperate to bleed her once again for his own
relief. Dolley only heard of his wild behavior after he had
departed again in futile rage, and she wrote to him in deep distress, offering to raffle off some of her remaining possessions,
such as Stuart portraits, for his benefit.

He did not bother to reply. The trustees got wind of her
proposal, and were horrified, and quickly put a stop to that.

The procession of presidents continued through the background of Dolley's life. General Zachary Taylor, hero of the
Mexican War, was the eleventh since Washington. He was a
man of no political experience, and his wife was another who
shirked her official duties. On New Year's Day, 1849, Dolley's
house overflowed as usual. She felt younger, and at peace, now

that her great task was accomplished and the papers were in safekeeping. She looked well, she presided with her usual grace and charm, and except that she seemed always to have been there, nobody thought of her age.

She had made no will, because for so long she had had almost nothing to leave besides the precious papers. Now, with the trust fund in her name, she was faced by that dismal duty. She discussed it with Richard Cutts's older brother—she wanted to provide for the devoted Annie, her companion since Madison's death thirteen years before, by dividing the money equally between her and Payne, while everything else was to go to Payne, almost doubling his inheritance. At the same time, she seemed troubled and uncertain, and out of consideration for her Cutts did not press the matter. It never occurred to anyone that once her stabilized financial situation became known to Payne's creditors he would be pressed for reassurance as to his ultimate prospects.

In June he suddenly appeared in Lafayette Square and demanded that she make a will in his favor, naming him sole heir. Now. At once. He drew it up in his own handwriting, ready for her to sign. She had numbers of friends in Washington who would have come to her within minutes if she had sent a note requesting their presence, but she allowed him to produce his own witnesses. They were strangers to her. She signed her name where they told her to, as though in a daze, and the signature was tremulous. It was altogether a sordid, humiliating business for her, conducted in a flurry of haste and secrecy. She was stunned by this final evidence of her son's irresponsible, unfeeling greed.

Then she was ill. At first it seemed nothing serious, but she was brooding. People dropped in to see her and try to cheer her up, without knowing what lay on her mind—among them Mary Cutts, and her old friend Eliza Collins Lee. She was not herself, they could see. She sent for Cutts and confessed to him that she had signed Payne's document, and asked him to draw up another will along the lines she had discussed with him before Payne arrived. When Cutts brought it to her bedside she was so weak that she had to be lifted up to sign it. Mrs. Lee was still there as a witness. They reminded her that the last will signed was always the one. She said she knew it. She had found the strength to deny Payne his way for once, and Annie was provided for.

After a few more days of fading consciousness she died, on July 12, 1849. It is possible that Payne Todd's last visit to Lafayette Square had finally broken the heart that had always been so light.

Bibliography

Adams, J. T. *The Living Jefferson*. 1936.

American Church. Edited by Vergilius Ferm. 1953.

Anthony, Katherine. *Dolly Madison*. 1949.

Appleton's Cyclopedia of American Biography. 1898.

Brant, Irving. *James Madison*. 6 vols., 1941–61.

Burr's Private Journals. Edited by E. W. Bixby. 1903.

Burt, Struthers. *Philadelphia: Holy Experiment*. 1945.

Chinard, Gilbert. *Thomas Jefferson*. 1939.

Chinard, Gilbert. *Honest John Adams*. 1933.

Chitwood, Oliver P. *John Tyler*. 1939.

Clark, A. C. *Dolly Madison*. 1914.

Clark, A. C. *Greenleaf and Law in Washington*. 1901.

Clark, Bennett. *John Quincy Adams*. 1932.

Cresson, W. P. *James Monroe*. 1946.

Cutts, L. B. *Memoirs and Letters of Dolly Madison*. 1886.

Dean, E. L. *Dolly Madison*. 1928.

Ellet, E. F. *Court Circles of the Republic*. 1872.

Encyclopedia of Religion. Edited by Vergilius Ferm. 1945.

Fuess, C. M. *Daniel Webster*. 2 vols. 1930.

Goodwin, Maude Wilder. *Dolly Madison*. 1898.

Green, Constance. *Washington: Village and Capitol*. 1962.

Guide to American Religions. Edited by Leo Rosten. 1955.

Hamlin, Talbot. *Benjamin Latrobe*. 1955.

Hazleton, George. *National Capitol*. 1914.

Herron, Paul. *Story of Capitol Hill*. 1963.

Hunt, Gaillard. *James Madison.* 1902.

———. *Life in America 100 Years Ago.* 1914.

Hurd, Charles. *Washington Cavalcade.* 1948.

———. *The White House.* 1940.

James, Marquis. *Andrew Jackson.* 1940.

Lossing, Benjamin. *War of 1812.* 1869.

Lynch, Denis Tilden. *Martin Van Buren and His Times.* 1929.

Parmet, H. S. and Hecht, M. B. *Aaron Burr.* 1967.

Diary of James K. Polk. Edited by Allan Nevens. 1929.

Protestant Dictionary. Edited by Vergilius Ferm. 1951.

Repplier, Agnes. *Philadelphia.* 1898.

Schachner, Nathan. *Aaron Burr.* 1937.

Smith, Mrs. Harrison. *The First Forty Years of Washington Society.* Edited by Gaillard Hunt. 1906.

Stevens, W. O. *Washington, D.C.* 1943.

Tucker, Glenn. *Poltroons and Patriots.* 2 vols. 1954.

U.S. Capitol Historical Society. *We, the People: Story of the U.S. Capitol.* 1963.

Watson, J. F. *Annals of Philadelphia.* 1830.

Westcott, Thompson. *Historic Mansions of Philadelphia.* 1877.

Wheatley, Vera. *Harriet Martineau.* 1957.

White House Historical Association. *The White House.* 1962.

W. P. A. Guide to Washington, D.C. 1937.

Index